A MIDDLE CLASS WITHOUT DEMOCRACY

D1507856

A Middle Class without Democracy

Economic Growth and the Prospects for Democratization in China

Jie Chen

OXFORD
UNIVERSITY PRESS

OXFORD
UNIVERSITY PRESS

Oxford University Press is a department of the University of Oxford.
It furthers the University's objective of excellence in research, scholarship,
and education by publishing worldwide.

Oxford   New York
Auckland   Cape Town   Dar es Salaam   Hong Kong   Karachi
Kuala Lumpur   Madrid   Melbourne   Mexico City   Nairobi
New Delhi   Shanghai   Taipei   Toronto

With offices in
Argentina   Austria   Brazil   Chile   Czech Republic   France   Greece
Guatemala   Hungary   Italy   Japan   Poland   Portugal   Singapore
South Korea   Switzerland   Thailand   Turkey   Ukraine   Vietnam

Oxford is a registered trade mark of Oxford University Press
in the UK and certain other countries.

Published in the United States of America by
Oxford University Press
198 Madison Avenue, New York, NY 10016

Library of Congress Cataloging-in-Publication Data
Chen, Jie.
A middle class without democracy : economic growth and the prospects for
democratization in China / Jie Chen.
      p. cm.
Includes bibliographical references and index.
ISBN 978–0–19–984163–9 (hardcover); 978–0–19–938561–4 (paperback)
1. Middle class—China—History—21st century.
2. Economic development—China—History—21st century.
3. China—Politics and government—21st century.
4. Democracy—China—History—21st century.   I. Title.
HT690.C55C3954 2013
305.5'50951—dc23

To Yanping and Jackie

Contents

Tables and Figures

Tables

Figures

Preface

SINCE THE MID-1990S, I have witnessed many of my friends and family members in China miraculously move from their pre-reform status of "proletariat" to their current status of "middle class." Now they lead their lives in ways that are very similar to those of the middle class in the United States and other industrialized countries. For example, they drive their own cars, own or rent their own apartments, have respectable jobs that require at least college degrees, engage in hobbies that are popular among the middle class in the West, and occasionally participate in local politics. I have been profoundly fascinated by what I have witnessed about the new middle class in China over these years and have constantly asked myself and others some "burning" questions about this new social class. How can we best characterize and define this new middle class in China? Is the new middle class in China the same as the middle class in the West? Can this social class play a crucial role in shaping the future of China? Is China's middle class going to be supportive of political changes toward democracy in this undemocratic country, where the Chinese Communist Party (CCP) has kept a firm grip on political power for more than half a century?

To seek answers to these intriguing questions, about five years ago I embarked on this research project about the role of the new middle class in democratization in China. Over the course of the project, I have learned much about this topic that I could never have imagined. Even at the very beginning of this book, therefore, I cannot help but highlight one of the most intimate yet pivotal findings from the project: that is, the new middle class in China that began to emerge in the 1990s is very different from the middle classes in the West, although all these middle classes share some commonalities. The main difference is that China's new middle class has so far relied heavily on the state under the CCP or the party-state for its survival and growth since its birth. Due to this difference, as well as other factors, most members of the new middle class in China now are not in favor of political changes for democracy, changes that could no doubt threaten the very existence of the current party-state. With great enthusiasm, however, I also want to report that this social class may change its attitudinal and behavioral orientations toward democratization in China, once its dependence on the party-state decreases significantly. I hope that these findings, along with others presented in this book, may contribute to our understanding of China's new middle class in general and its role in potential political changes in particular. I also hope that many outside of academe—such as policy makers, business leaders and practitioners, and general readers who are interested in China—will find the results presented in this book useful and interesting.

In the entire process of this research project, I was so fortunate as to be helped and supported by many people and several institutions. Without their help and support, I would not have been able to accomplish this project. First and foremost, I would like to express my heartfelt gratitude to those people who provided me with insightful guidance, abundant encouragement, and generous assistance at various stages of the research project. Particularly, my gratitude goes to Lei Tao of the Beijing Academy of Social Sciences and Yiyin Yang of the Chinese Academy of Social Sciences for helping me design and implement the probability-sample survey of three major cities—Beijing, Chengdu, and Xi'an—in China, and Lu Chunlong of the China University of Politics and Law for his crucial assistance in conducting the in-depth interviews of over 200 residents in those three cities. This book is written based on data collected from the probability-sample survey and the in-depth interviews. I want to thank Bruce Dickson, David Earnest, David S. G. Goodman, Cheng Li, Chunlin Li, Lianjiang Li, Melanie Manion, Kevin O'Brien, Dorothy Solinger, Wenfang Tang, Kellee S. Tsai, Xiaojin Zhang, Yang Zhong, and Xiaohong Zhou for their critical and constructive comments on arguments and methods in the earlier versions of this book. These invaluable comments, which were provided either at conferences and symposia or through correspondence over the years, enabled me to improve many aspects of this book. I am also heavily indebted to my friend, Robert Holden, for meticulously editing an early draft of my work, and my research assistant, Narisong Huhe, for skillfully helping me conduct various statistical analyses for this book.

This research project was also supported by several institutions. Acknowledgements are due to the National Science Foundation (NSF) for providing a generous research grant (SES-0550518/0936245) to support my research for this book. Any opinions, findings, and conclusions presented in this book are those of this author and do not necessarily reflect the views of the NSF. Here I would like to thank my grant officer at the NSF, Brian Humes, for going out of his way to help me deal with challenges and contingencies in working with various research institutions in China. He has been one of the most effective and helpful grant officers I have ever worked with in my entire academic career. Also, I greatly appreciate my previous home institution, Old Dominion University, for granting me research leaves, and my current home institution, the University of Idaho, for providing me with a research assistant for this project.

My sincere gratitude certainly goes to David McBride, my editor at Oxford University Press, for his enthusiastic support for and insightful guidance on this project. He was one of the few editors who first discovered the significance of this research in social sciences, as well as in China studies. His optimistic and constructive attitude inspired me to strive for the best in my research for this book. I wish that every serious author in the field could be fortunate enough to find and work with an editor like David McBride.

Parts of this book were published in my previous works as follows: 2011, "Democratization and the Middle Class in China: The Middle Class's Attitudes toward Democracy," *Political Research Quarterly* (SAGE Publisher) 64 (3): 705–719; 2010, "Attitudes toward Democracy and the Political Behavior of China's Middle Class," in *China's Emerging Middle Class: Beyond Economic Transformation*, ed. Cheng Li, Brookings Institution Press: 334–358; 2002, "Why Do People Vote in Semicompetitive Elections in China?" *Journal of Politics* (Cambridge University Press) 64: 178–197. Permissions were granted by these publishers for using the aforementioned works in this book.

Last but not least, I want to take this opportunity to express many thanks to my wife and daughter for willingly accommodating my research activities for this book, activities that very often compete with my obligations to my family as husband and father. Both of them forwent many vacations and planned family events because of my research for this project. For all these years, neither has been adequately compensated for the sacrifice she has endured for this project, as well as my professional career. As I am deeply indebted to each of them, therefore, I dedicate this book to my wife, Yanping, and my daughter, Jackie.

Jie Chen
August 1, 2012

Abbreviations

CCP	Chinese Communist Party
CPPCC	Chinese People's Political Consultative Conference
CRC	Community residential committee
CRS	Contract responsibility system
EAB	East Asian barometer
ELI	Export-led industrialization
ETDZ	Economic and technological development zone
FDI	Foreign direct investment
HOA	Homeowners' associations
ISI	Import substitution industrialization
NPC	National People's Congress
OLS	Ordinary least square (statistical model)
PRC	People's Republic of China
RMB	*Renminbi* ("people's currency": the official currency of the People's Republic of China)
SEZ	Special economic zone
SOE	State-owned enterprise
TVE	Township and village enterprise

A MIDDLE CLASS WITHOUT DEMOCRACY

Introduction: The Contingent Middle Class

SINCE THE EARLY 1990s, I have undertaken field research in various parts of China every year. On each trip, I have been struck by the fact that more and more people, especially those in urban areas, live their lives in ways that increasingly resemble those of the middle class in the United States. Perfect examples of this social phenomenon are four friends of mine, who have lived and worked in China their entire lifetimes. All four today have typically middle-class occupations: department director (*chuzhang*) in the Beijing Municipality, midlevel manager of a reputable computer company, business/financial lawyer practicing with a private law firm, and a well-established freelance music composer. All four own their own moderate apartments in trendy areas of Beijing and drive their own, mid-priced cars. They invest tremendous energy and resources in the education of their children. Last but not least, each of them is well informed about international affairs—especially major political events and issues in the United States and the Middle East—as well as China's domestic affairs.

As Chinese society has become increasingly modernized in the past three decades, the new *middle class*[1] of people like my four friends has steadily emerged as a salient socioeconomic and sociopolitical force. According to the most recent nationwide, representative-sample survey conducted by the Chinese Academy of Social Sciences (CASS), the middle class accounted for 15% and 23% of the total population in China in 2000 and 2006, respectively (Lu 2002, 2010). The former vice minister of Foreign Trade and Economic Cooperation and chief trade representative of the People's Republic China (PRC) predicted that in 2010 the size of the middle class would reach 30% of the population (see Zhou 2005, 1). Some economists even forecast that the middle class in China will constitute 74% of the population by 2030: "the majority of Chinese could go from being poor to being the middle class" (Kharas and Gertz 2010, 43). There is little doubt that the sheer size and sociopolitical influence of the Chinese middle class will continue to grow rapidly as China continues to modernize.

What kind of role can the new middle class be expected to play in the political changes favoring democracy in China? Is this new social class capable of thinking and acting *democratically,* and if so, might it serve as the harbinger of democratization, as many in the West expect? Given the saliency of the emergence and growth of the new middle class, political scientists and other China watchers have become more and more interested in these questions (e.g., Glassman 1991; Solinger 1992, 2008; Goodman 1996, 1999; Chen 2002; Xiao 2003; He Li 2003; O'Brien and Stern 2008; Zhang 2010).[2] However, their answers to these important questions do not as yet point to a consensus on the role of the middle class in a democratic transition or the attitudinal/behavioral orientations of middle-class individuals to various political issues. Furthermore, almost no representative- or probability-sample study has ever systematically addressed these questions. To answer these critical and timely questions, this book systematically examines the extent, sociopolitical sources, and behavioral consequences of the new middle class's support for democratization and democracy itself. More important, the examination of these issues in this book draws on a unique set of data collected from a probability-sample survey and a series of in-depth interviews conducted in three major Chinese cities in late 2007 and early 2008. Such data will allow this study to provide a more robust test of various hypotheses or arguments from earlier studies regarding the middle class's democratic support in China, the largest yet most dynamic developing country.

Furthermore, the findings presented in this book will shed some new light on at least two other important issues related to the sources, behavioral consequences, and extent of the Chinese middle class's democratic support. First, since the size and power of the middle class continues to increase dramatically, we can expect that the findings about this class's attitudes toward democracy will help us better understand the future trajectory of political changes—particularly those potentially leading toward democracy—in China. Such an improved understanding of the political trends will in turn assist political leaders worldwide in designing and implementing policies to cope with future political changes in this increasingly influential country.

Second, because China is still considered an undemocratic, developing country, the findings regarding the Chinese middle class's democratic support will undoubtedly have significant implications for studies of the role of the middle classes in democratization in other undemocratic, developing countries. Such implications from this study of China's middle class will further contribute to general theoretical inquiry into the role of the middle classes as forces supporting or opposing democracy in the developing world.

In this chapter, I will discuss the theoretical approach and the analytical framework that guide my investigation of support for democracy by China's middle class and then describe the empirical data on which this study is based. A brief summary of each chapter will follow.

I. "Unilinear" Approach Versus "Contingent" Approach

There is a large body of literature on the orientation of the middle class toward democracy and democratization. Within this general literature, there seem to be two distinct approaches. One can be considered a "unilinear"[3] approach (Lipset 1959, 1981; Lipset and Bendix 1959; Nie, Powell, and Prewitt 1969; Dahl 1971; Luebbert 1991; Huntington 1991; Glassman 1997). Closely associated with modernization theory, this approach emphasizes the relationship between economic modernization and political democratization. It contends that as modernization unfolds in a society, the levels of the individual's income, education, socioeconomic mobility, and valuation of freedom markedly increase. All these attributes in turn promote democratization in a non-democratic society and strengthen democratic institutions in a democratic society. According to this approach, importantly, "the rising middle class *universally* embodies these [attributes]" and serves as the "main thrust of the democratization movement" (Hattori, Funatsu, and Torii 2003, 129–130). Such an approach suggests a set of unilinear causal relationships: socioeconomic modernization gives rise to the middle class, which in turn spearheads democratization in a non-democratic society. In other words, like Barrington Moore's (1966) famous thesis of "no bourgeois, no democracy,"[4] this approach suggests that the middle class usually serves as a strong supporter of democratization and democracy.

Proponents of this approach also argue that unlike individuals in the upper class who have abundant economic resources and close ties as clients to political elites, those in the middle class have limited economic resources and lack connections with powerful patrons in the government. Out of self-interest, therefore, the middle class supports a democratic system in which their individual rights and modest property holdings may best be protected from potential encroachment by the government and the upper class (Glassman 1995, 1997). In addition, some of these scholars contend from the socio-behavioral perspective that middle-class individuals tend to favor democracy because, compared to lower class individuals, they have enough education and leisure time to enable them to understand and participate in public affairs effectively (Mills 1953; Lane 1959).

This approach has been supported by evidence from studies on the role of the middle classes in the transition toward or maintenance of democracy *mainly* in the West (e.g., Eulau 1956a, 1956b; Lipset 1959, 1981; Nie et al. 1969; Dahl 1971; Milbrath 1977; Glassman 1995, 1997; Walsh, Jennings, and Stoker 2004).[5] These studies find that middle-class individuals usually support democratic principles and take action in support of the rise and/or maintenance of a democratic system and against a non-democratic system.

The other approach may be referred to as a "contingent" approach (Johnson 1985; Stephens 1989; Rueschemeyer, Stephens, and Stephens 1992; Bertrand 1998; Jones 1998; Englehart 2003; Hsiao and Koo 1997; Koo 1991; Brown and Jones 1995; Bell 1998; Acemoglu and Robinson 2000; Bellin 2000; Hattori and Funatsu 2003; Thompson 2004). Unlike the unilinear approach, which is based on the premise of the unilinear causality between modernization and democracy, the contingent approach in general assumes that the relationship between economic development and democratization can be best characterized as dynamic. As Bruce Dickson (2003, 12) argues, "democratization is not a natural result of economic growth, it is a political process fraught with conflict, negotiations, and occasionally setbacks." Based on their study of the most recent political changes in post-communist Europe and Eurasia, some analysts also contend that development does not necessarily lead to a "cross-national spread of democratic orders"; instead, it sometimes is followed by various dictatorships (Bunce, McFaul, and Stoner-Weiss 2010). In addition, while the unilinear approach strongly implies the almost inevitable prodemocracy stance of the middle class as the causal effect of modernization, the contingent approach suggests that the orientation of the middle class toward democracy is contingent upon some salient sociopolitical and socioeconomic conditions. These conditions vary with the political contexts of different countries and with economic development stages within each country. Such conditions or factors include, but are not limited to, the middle class's dependence on (or independence from) the state, its perceived socioeconomic well-being, its political alliance with other classes (e.g., upper or working classes), its own class cohesiveness (or fragmentation), and its fear of political instability. In a nutshell, proponents of the contingent approach contend that the middle class does not necessarily support democratization, especially when it is heavily dependent upon or closely associated with the authoritarian state, socially/materially well off or satisfied, fragmented as a class, and/or worried about political instability. In other words, as all or some of these conditions change, the middle class in a given society will shift its orientation toward democratization and democracy accordingly. As Hagen Koo (1991, 506) argues, therefore, "it would not make much sense...to characterize [the middle class] as progressive or conservative" in a permanent sense.

Unlike the unilinear approach, the contingent approach has been supported by the evidence from studies of the middle class mainly in developing countries, especially those that undergo rapid economic transformations (e.g., Koo 1991; Rueschemeyer et al. 1992; Brown and Jones 1995; Rodan 1993; Johnson 1985; Bell 1998; Jones 1998; Lam 1999; Torii 2003; Englehart 2003). Most of these studies find that the middle classes take different stances toward democratization, and the variation in the stances results from the middle classes' relationships with the state, evaluations of social and economic life, and fear of sociopolitical instability. In addition, adherents of the contingent approach discover that various subgroups of the middle classes may acquire different attitudes toward democracy, as they are variably affected by socioeconomic conditions.

While not all of the studies mentioned previously perfectly fit either of the two approaches, one can still discern two *distinct* underlying logics within the literature. On the one hand, based on the premise of the unilinear causality between modernization and democratization/democracy, the unilinear approach argues for the near inevitability of the middle class's democratic support. On the other hand, rooted in the assumption of the dynamic relationship between economic development and democratization, the contingent approach calls attention to the contingency of the middle class's attitudes toward democracy.

II. The Middle Class and Democracy in Developing Countries

Which of these two approaches—the unilinear approach or the contingent approach—seems to be more pertinent to the middle classes in developing countries, especially those in the process of profound economic transformation such as China? A brief survey of the middle classes in these countries seems to provide plausible evidence that supports the contingent approach. It shows a wide variation of the middle classes' orientations toward democracy: the middle classes have at some times and in some countries supported democratization and democracy but at other times and in other countries backed authoritarian regimes (or rulers).

In East/Southeast Asia (e.g., Koo 1991; Brown and Jones 1995; Jones 1998; Bertrand 1998; Englehart 2003; Kimura 2003; So 2004), the middle classes seemed to be quite ambivalent toward democracy and democratization and had vested interests in the continuity and stability of authoritarian rule since they were the main beneficiaries of state-led economic growth in the past decades (Bell 1998). In Singapore, the majority of the middle class accepted the undemocratic government as long as it continued to satisfy its material needs (Lam 1999; Rodan 1993). In Malaysia, the burgeoning middle class, especially ethnic Malays, either actively supported an increasingly authoritarian state or remained politically apathetic (Bell 1998; Jones 1998; Torii 2003). In Indonesia, the new middle class stood firmly on the side of the status quo (Bell 1998; Jones 1998). In Thailand, the new middle class was ambivalent toward democracy, like the middle classes of other Southeast Asian countries (Englehart 2003). Even in now-democratic Taiwan and South Korea, the new middle classes were often ambivalent toward democracy and did little to stimulate democratization, as their class interests were often tied to those of state elites (Brown and Jones 1995; Lu 1991; Jones 1998; Hsiao 2010; Han 2010), while the working classes—especially in South Korea—played a decisive role in democratization (see, e.g., Rueschemeyer et al. 1992, 294).

In the second-largest developing country, India, the middle class's "commitment to principles of democracy is weak" (Gupta 2000, 10) or ambivalent at best. The new middle class in that country has been "advocating liberty *and* authoritarianism, equality *and* hierarchy, all at the same time" (Baviskar and Ray 2011, 6). In the era of economic reform, many members of the Indian middle class even turned their backs on the existing democracy, contending that India "needs a dictator." They did so especially when they perceived that "their interests [were] not being served by politicians and by the state" (Fernandes 2004, 186–187) and their privileged status was threatened by the lower class (see, e.g., Baviskar and Ray 2011). Nonetheless, as Leela Fernandes points out, the state continued to play a "significant role" in shaping the political attitudes and behavior of India's new middle class.

In Latin America, the middle classes were also "frequently ambivalent concerning democracy" (e.g., Rueschemeyer et al. 1992, 167). As Dietrich Rueshmemeyer and his associates pointed out, "the ambivalent attitude of the middle classes towards democracy became clear in their frequent acceptance of restricted democracy as well as in their repeated support for coups overthrowing democratic regimes" (Rueschemeyer et al. 1992, 222). For instance, the middle classes used to ally with sectors of the upper classes and the military, and eventually helped in the installation of authoritarian regimes in Brazil, Argentina, and other Latin American countries during the 1970s (see, e.g., Rueschemeyer et al. 1992; Owensby 1999). According to these scholars, such ambivalence or contingence of the orientations toward democracy within the middle classes of Latin America was caused by several key sociopolitical factors unique to that region, such as the type of economic development strategies pursued by the states, the middle classes' self-interests, the nature of political allies available to the middle classes, cultural acceptance of social hierarchy and patronage, and the roles of the states of those late developers—which were more prominent than those in early industrializers in shaping each new social class and its political alliances.

In sum, the comparative survey of the middle classes in developing countries, as presented previously, clearly indicates that the middle classes' attitudinal and behavioral orientations toward democratization and democracy do vary with geographical and temporal differences. Such a wide variation has apparently been caused by the contingency of the middle classes' orientations toward democratization and democracy. More important, this contingency seems to result from several key socioeconomic and political conditions that are considered unique to the developing countries (or late and late-late developers, which will be defined later in this chapter). One of these conditions or factors is the prominent role played by the states in these countries—particularly during the major socioeconomic transformations—in creating and shaping the new social classes, such as the new middle classes, new entrepreneurs, and new working classes. Such a prominent role of the states in the developing countries has often been manifested as a national strategy of state-led economic development. To take one example, the strategies of import substitute industrialization (ISI) versus export-led industrialization (ELI) have had significant impacts on the relationships between the new middle classes and the states, and hence the middle classes' orientation toward democratization and democracy (and the current political regimes). This type of relationship between the middle class and state seems to be the case for almost all the developing countries in East Asia, Southeast Asia, South Asia, and Latin America, which were surveyed previously.

Another critical condition for the contingency of the middle classes' orientations toward democratization and democracy, based on the previous comparative survey, seems to be the constant shifts of the middle classes' self-interest in response to the performance of the incumbent governments and their own well-being. As mentioned earlier, many in the middle class in India turned their backs on the existing democratic institutions because they at times perceived their self-interest to be adversely affected by the incumbent public policies, even though the policies had been made through democratic procedures (e.g., Fernandes 2004; Baviskar and Ray 2011). The middle classes in Latin American countries from time to time sided with the upper classes and the military juntas in support of the authoritarian regimes, simply for the protection of their own sociopolitical and socioeconomic interests, such as their inclusion in the political power structure and economic well-being (e.g., Rueschemeyer et al. 1992, chapter 5).

Based on the results of the comparative survey of the middle classes' attitudinal and behavioral orientations toward democratization and democracy in developing countries (or late developers), one may conclude that the contingent approach seems to be the more relevant and suitable theoretical framework to explain the middle class's stances toward democracy in authoritarian developing countries, such as China. Moreover, the findings from this study of middle-class support for democratization in China may have some important implications for the study of the middle classes in other developing countries, since China shares many sociopolitical and socioeconomic commonalities with those developing countries surveyed earlier, such as a position of late development in the global economy and the strong role of the state in socioeconomic transformations. On the other hand, this comparative survey in turn suggests that the unilinear approach claiming that "a growing middle class creates pressure for democracy is tenuous at best" (Bertrand 1998, 356) for the studies of the middle classes' orientations toward democratization and democracy in the developing world.

III. The Analytical Framework

China not only is a developing country but also is a Leninist, authoritarian one where the sole legal political party,[6] the Chinese Communist Party (CCP), still largely controls society. The CCP-led state has played a preponderant role in the extraordinary economic transformation that China has been experiencing in the past three decades. These fundamental attributes of China's current socioeconomic and sociopolitical conditions facilitate a decisive role for the state in creating and shaping new social classes, including the new middle class. Following the contingent approach as delineated earlier, therefore, one can assume that the new middle class in China is dependent upon the state for its rise and growth and shares common values with the state.

Based on this assumption, the analytical framework in this study is not only induced by the contingent approach but also informed by two related theoretical traditions. These two traditions include the late-development notion (see, e.g., Gerschenkron 1962) and the state-centered paradigm (see, e.g., Evans, Rueschemeyer, and Skocpol 1985; Evans 1995). While these theoretical traditions—especially the state-centered paradigm—have drawn some criticisms over the years,[7] both traditions have been continuously applied in various studies of economic and political development in developing countries.[8] Instead of entering the debate over these two traditions, I draw some useful insights from both of them for my study of the middle class's democratic support within the context of late development.

A. The State and Late Development

In his seminal collection of essays, *Economic Backwardness in Historical Perspective*, Alexander Gerschenkron (1962) first established the critical notion of "late developer" economic development, which has helped many social scientists understand socioeconomic development in contemporary developing countries. According to Gerschenkron, the "late developers" are those countries that joined the global tide of development when it was already in rapid motion. As a result, developing countries such as China and newly industrialized countries can be considered late developers, since they commenced their processes of economic development when economic development was already in rapid motion or reached maturity in Western Europe and North America. Moreover, it is contended that late developers do not follow the early industrializers' "spontaneous" model in their economic development (Kohli 2004, 8). Particularly, Gerschenkron (1962, 6) unequivocally disputes modernization theory,[9] which suggests that the history of the advanced countries has "[traced] out the road of development for the [currently] more backward countries." He instead argues that the economic development of the late-developing countries by "the very virtue of their backwardness" will differ fundamentally from that of the early-industrialized countries (Gerschenkron 1962, 7).

Because of such socioeconomic "backwardness," late developers have faced challenges that have set them apart from early industrializers. These challenges are manifested in at least two major areas. First, all the late developers lack capital, a trained workforce, and advanced technologies when they initiate major economic development programs (see also Kohli 2004). In addition, as Packenham (1992) pointed out, they all face a very peculiar international economic condition,[10] which could trap them in unfavorable positions in the transnational division of labor. Second, to avoid being left further behind early-industrialized countries or losing chances for development altogether, late developers must overcome such socioeconomic backwardness and disadvantages within a *shorter* time period than that in which early-industrialized countries had to overcome similar obstacles.

Due to these peculiar challenges faced by late developers, Gerschenkron (1962) added, the states in these countries normally play a more important role than do the states in early-industrial-ized countries in the process of socioeconomic development. This is mainly because late-developing countries need a strong state to meet those challenges effectively under time pressure. For instance, a late developer needs a strong state to pool the country's resources and mobilize its population to compensate for the inadequate supplies of capital, entrepreneurship, and techno-logical capacity within a constrained timeframe to catch up and compete with developed countries. Meanwhile, a strong state is needed to design and coordinate strategies to cope with unprec-edented, severe international economic competition. As Vivek Chibber (2003, 13) concisely sums up, therefore,

> the phenomenon of the late development...has typically been associated with an important role for the state. This was, of course, true for the initial batch of countries, such as Germany and Japan, attempting to catch up with their more advanced competitors; it has been even more so for what Albert Hirschman calls the "late late developers"—the nations across the South in the post-war twentieth century that undertook programs of development planning.

B. The Capacities of the State

Gerschenkron's argument on the role of the state in a late-developing country has been enriched and applied to con-temporary studies of the states in developing countries (late developers) by state-centered scholars who try to bring the state back into the central place of political analysis (e.g., Evans et al. 1985; Evans 1995). Their studies of state autonomy and capaci-ties are consistent with the kernel of Gerschenkron's original argument on the role of the state and help advance our under-standing of the states in the contemporary developing world.

In terms of the autonomy of the state, contemporary state-centered analysts have in effect developed Gerschenkron's

argument for the *desirability* of a strong state into an argument
for the inherent *autonomy* of the state. As Theda Skocpol (1985, 9)
argues, "states conceived as organizations claiming control over
territories and people may formulate and pursue goals that are
not simply reflective of the demands or interests of social groups,
classes, or society." This kind of autonomy is derived not only from
"the basic need to maintain control and order" in crises or major
socioeconomic transformations but also from the fact that only
organizationally coherent collectivities of state officials, relatively
insulated from societal forces, are likely to launch distinctive state
strategies in times of major socioeconomic change. "Likewise, collectivities of officials may elaborate already established public
policies in distinctive ways, acting relatively continuously over
long stretches of time" (Skocpol 1985, 9). To Gerschenkron's argument for the necessity of a strong role for the state in major socioeconomic transformation, contemporary state-centered scholars
added empirical and theoretical support, especially by developing
the idea of state autonomy. They suggested that the state in a late
developer not only *should*—as Gerschenkron argued—but also *can*
play an active and decisive role in the nation's social, economic,
and political life due to its structural autonomy.

As for the capacities of the state to realize any goal it may pursue,
contemporary state-centered analysts also provide us with some
very useful insights about resources, dimensions, and strengths
of such capacities (e.g., Skocpol 1985; Amsden 1985; Katzenstein
1985; Tilly 1985; Stepan 1985; Rueschemeyer and Evans 1985;
Evans 1995). Among all other resources of state capacities, these
scholars particularly emphasize the importance of financial and
organizational ones. The financial resources under the state's control, as Skocpol (1985, 17) points out, serve as the critical material
base on which the state can fulfill various basic tasks, such as
those "to employ personnel, to co-op political support, to subsidize
economic enterprises, and to fund social programs." The organizational resources are considered as a set of *cohesive* "organizational
configurations" within the state apparatus, which together "affect

political culture, encourage some kinds of group formation and collective political actions (but not others), and make possible the raising of certain political issues (but not others)" (Skocpol 1985, 21) and effectively intervene and coordinate socioeconomic transformations (or reforms) (Rueschemeyer and Evans 1985).

According to the contemporary state-centered approach, state capacities may be examined and gauged along two dimensions (see Chibber 2003, 7). One is the *cohesiveness* of the state as a strategic actor in formulating and implementing national policies (Evans 1995). The other dimension is the ability of the state to mobilize and guide societal forces for the achievement of national goals (Amsden 1989. In short, these two dimensions together are indicative of the state's ability to formulate and implement policy and to control socioeconomic and political forces in society. Thus, the results of the role played by the state may be in large part gauged along these two dimensions of the state's capacities.

In terms of the strength of state capacities, the contemporary state-centered scholars focus on the *effectiveness* of the state in affecting various areas of socioeconomic and political life. Such effectiveness is often measured by the concrete impacts of state interventions on society. In addition, there appear two different yet complementary trends of analysis of effectiveness among these scholars. Some of them tend to emphasize the variation in effectiveness of interventions by state organizations in various policy areas *within* a country (e.g., Rueschemeyer and Evans 1985; Skocpol 1985). Others seek to compare and contrast the effectiveness of the states' interventions in major socioeconomic transformations *across* countries (e.g., Wade 1990; Woo-Cumings 1999; Chibber 2003; Kohli 2004). They suggest that an effective intervention of the state has been a key ingredient of rapid economic development, especially in parts of East Asia. For example, some of them pointed out that the Korean and Taiwanese states had successfully intervened in international trade and currency exchange rates, as well as the price structure of the domestic economy (Luedde-Neurath 1988; White and Wade 1988; Amsden 1989); they were also active in directing the structure of private investment (Wade 1990).

All in all, the combination of the Gerschenkronian notion of late development and the contemporary state-centered approach yields a theoretical foundation on which to base the forthcoming analysis. In a nutshell, this theoretical foundation establishes the connection between the socioeconomic conditions of late development and the degree of state intervention in major socioeconomic transformations: that is, the socioeconomic conditions of a late developer *necessitate* a strong role for the state in its search for rapid socioeconomic development, and the autonomy and capacities of the state may *facilitate* such a strong role. This conceptual connection is relevant to our study because it largely resonates with the strong role played by the state in China. It can be said that to compensate for the typical disadvantages of a late developer, the Chinese state needs to play a strong role in leading the unprecedented post-Mao socioeconomic transformation. Moreover, the Chinese state has been to a large extent able to play such a proactive leadership role in initiating and guiding this transformation because it enjoys high levels of autonomy and capacities.

It is also worth noting that compared to the states of many other late developers, the Chinese state is likely to have even stronger capacities to penetrate society in general and to guide economic transformations. From the state-centered perspective mentioned earlier, such capacities are mainly derived from two sources: the state's control over national financial resources and the state's somewhat monolithic organizational configurations, which have been created and controlled by the single Leninist party. In addition, as Peter Evans (1985, 59) points out, "the historical character of the bureaucratic apparatus must be taken into account in any attempt to explain its capacity, or lack of capacity, to intervene." Thus, the more than half a century of totalitarian and authoritarian rule under the Chinese Communist Party has also reinforced such a strong role and the dominance of the state in Chinese society.

C. The Role of the State in Creating and Shaping Social Classes

Some analysts of social classes in developing countries argue that through its active and effective interventions in various areas of economic and political life, the state in a developing country also plays a decisive role in creating social classes, such as the new entrepreneurs and the new middle classes, and hence in shaping their socioeconomic and political traits (Pearson 1997; Bell 1998; Jones 1998; Shin 1999; Bellin 2000, 2002; Chibber 2003; Dickson 2003, 2008; Tsai 2005, 2006; Zhou 2004). As Dale Johnson (1985, 15) points out,

> in less developed societies the state tends to grow to the limits of resources that can be taxed or otherwise appropriated by government.... In part, this overdevelopment compensates for the presence of weak classes of local capitalists, or even their virtual nonexistence: states assume entrepreneurial functions, giving birth to technocratic, managerial, and technical groupings.

For instance, in the early stage of post-war economic development, the Korean state built government institutions not only to help indigenous capitalist classes grow but also to discipline them in national economic activities (Chibber 2003). The Taiwanese state implemented a series of policies simply to create and nurture a class of local private entrepreneurs in the early stage of Taiwan's post-war economic transformation, since such a class was almost nonexistent. In short, as some state-centered scholars explain (Evans et al. 1985, 253),

> the organizational arrangements of states, the existing patterns of state intervention in economic and social life, and policies already in place all influence the social interests [of classes] pursued in politics.... Some potential group identities are activated; others are not.

Following this particular theoretical line, some scholars further argue that the new social classes in a late-developing country not only are dependent upon the state for their rise and growth but also share with the state such interests as continuous economic growth and sociopolitical stability (or order). In a late-developing country, therefore, these new social classes are most likely to support the state and the political system sanctioned by the state (e.g., Pearson 1997; Bell 1998; Jones 1998; Shin 1999; Bellin 2000, 2002; Dickson 2003; Tsai 2005, 2006). More relevant to this study, for example, a group of scholars who have studied the role of the new private entrepreneurs in political change in China find that, due to their dependent and cooperative relationship with the state, these private entrepreneurs tend to be supportive of the incumbent CCP state and are less likely to be in favor of any political change in the current undemocratic political system (Pearson 1997; Dickson 2003; Tsai 2005, 2006).

D. The Role of the Middle Class in Democratization in the Developing World

What do the political orientations of the middle class in a late developer tend to be? Specifically, does the middle class think and act democratically in a late developer? Based on Gerschenkron's notion of late development and the contemporary state-centered paradigm, one may emphasize the vital role of the state in creating and shaping new social classes—including the new middle class, as well as indigenous private entrepreneurs—in late developers during rapid economic transformation and industrialization. Like new private entrepreneurs mentioned previously, a new middle class in a late-developing country not only is dependent upon the state for its rise and growth but also shares the common values already mentioned. In a late-developing country, therefore, the middle class is said to be most likely to support the state and the political system that is sanctioned by the state. Consequently, if the political system is undemocratic in that country, the middle class tends to turn its back on democratization to avoid antagonizing the state (Bell 1998; Brown and Jones 1995; Englehart 2003; Jones 1998; Shin 1999).

This argument about the role of the middle class in democratization in the late-developing countries has been supported by evidence from some empirical studies of the middle classes in other developing countries in East Asia, Southeast Asia, South Asia, and Latin America, as briefly mentioned earlier. Thus far, these studies provide empirical evidence to support the theoretical argument of the role of the middle class in undemocratic, developing countries.[11] Based on evidence from the developing societies, most of these studies suggest that the state often played a much more active role in creating and shaping the middle class in the late-developing world than it did in early-industrialized countries. The middle classes in those countries are "illiberal" or "undemocratic" and generally support the consolidation of authoritarian rule, because these middle classes are dependent upon state power for their own survival and prosperity during development (Bellin 2000, 2002; Bell 1998; Brown and Jones 1995; Englehart 2003; Johnson 1985; Jones 1998). This argument at least implies that even when the middle class becomes a majority of the population, this social class might still not be in favor of any drastic political change toward a democracy. This is because such a change may topple the current non-democratic regime and affect the very survival and prosperity of the middle class. As Diane E. Davis (2004, 345) concludes, therefore, "the general sense, then, has been that in any environment where a strong [non-democratic] state is necessary to jump-start or guide economic development, democracy will remain elusive."

In sum, following the contingent approach—mentioned earlier in this chapter—and drawing on the theoretical insights from both Gerschenkron's notion of late development and the contemporary state-centered paradigm, I assume that the Chinese state plays a critical role in molding the sociopolitical orientations of the new middle class, while such orientations are also contingent upon other salient socioeconomic and sociopolitical conditions at both the individual level (e.g., perceived social and economic well-being, and membership with the CCP) and the societal level (e.g., level and speed of local economic development). Moreover, I assume that the attitudinal orientations of the middle class significantly affect this class's political behavior (e.g., participating in local elections, petitioning the government). Following these assumptions, three key propositions for this inquiry can be derived:

(1) Compared to other social classes, particularly the lower class (who received less support and benefits from the party-state during the state-led, post-Mao reforms), the new Chinese middle class—especially those employed in the state apparatus—tends to be more supportive of the current party-state but less supportive of democratic changes that may directly challenge the state.

(2) The new middle class's attitudes toward democracy and the current party-state may be accounted for by this class's close ideational and institutional ties with the state and its perceived socioeconomic well-being, among other factors including its fear of political instability, its evaluations of governmental policies, and the perceived threat from other classes.

(3) The lack of support for democracy among the middle class tends to cause this social class to act in favor of the current state but in opposition to democratic changes.

These three hypotheses (or arguments) will be explored and tested against the data collected from the probability-sample survey and the set of in-depth interviews, which will be explained in the following section.

IV. Data

The data used in this study came from a probability-sample survey and a set of in-depth interviews (see Appendix), both of which were conducted in three Chinese cities, Beijing, Chengdu, and Xi'an, in late 2007 and early 2008. The general sociopolitical environment in China in the middle of the first decade of the twenty-first century when this survey was conducted can be characterized by several salient developments. They include the adoption of populist policies by the fourth generation of the CCP leadership under Hu Jintao to "build a harmonious society" (goujian hexie shehui) to quell dissatisfaction over worsening socioeconomic inequality and rampant official corruption; the central government's increased legal and constitutional protection for private property, which orthodox Marxism claimed was supposed to be eventually eliminated; and the party-state's stepped-up political repression for the sake of social stability while increasing economic freedom for private entrepreneurs, as well as ordinary citizens.

It is also worth mentioning some important sociopolitical conditions in the urban areas during the same time period: more and more urbanites became homeowners, while the frequency and severity of the conflicts between homeowners and real estate developers increased (Cai 2005); an increasing number of urban neighborhoods were incorporated into a new grassroots government system known as urban Community Residential Committees, which were supposed to be more democratically formed and run than their predecessors, Residential Committees (Derleth and Koldyk 2004); and, more important, the elections for the new people's deputies to the local people's congresses at the district level were conducted in major cities about one year before the probability-sample survey and in-depth interviews so that the respondents in the survey and interviews could still remember their involvement (or non-involvement) in these elections.[12]

All of these served as the underlying national and local sociopolitical conditions under which our survey and in-depth interviews were executed. The major procedures and components of the survey and the in-depth interviews, as well as the generalizability of the data from the survey, will be discussed as follows.

A. Representative Survey and In-Depth Interviews

This survey was conducted in three major cities in China, Beijing, Chengdu, and Xi'an, in cooperation with the Beijing Academy of Social Sciences (BASS), and China University of Politics and Law. The three cities were selected to represent approximately three distinct levels of economic development in urban China during the time of the survey. Beijing represents the most developed major urban areas in China, with per capita GDP over $7,000; Chengdu represents less developed major cities, with per capita GDP of around $4,000; Xi'an is indicative of the least developed major cities, with per capita GDP of about $2,000.

The survey was based on a probability sample of the general urban residents, aged 18 years and older, of each of the three cities. This probability sample was derived from a multistage sampling strategy. Three urban districts (*qu*) were randomly chosen at the first sampling stage in each city. In Beijing, the three districts were *Dongcheng, Haidian,* and *Chaoyang.* In Chengdu, the three districts were *Qingyang, Chenghua,* and *Wuhou.* In Xi'an, the three districts were *Lianhu, Xincheng,* and *Beilin.* At the second sampling stage, twelve streets (*jiedao*) were randomly selected from the three districts in each city, with four streets being selected from each district.[13] From each of the twelve streets in each city, four residents' communities were randomly chosen at the third stage of sampling, yielding a total of forty-eight residents' communities in each city. Then 1,200 households were randomly chosen from forty-eight residents' communities in each city by using the technique of probability proportionate to size (PPS). At this stage, the research team obtained the household registration list of each community from the street office in which the community was located. This process yielded a total of 3,600 households in three cities. At the final stage, one individual was chosen randomly from each of the 3,600 households as the interviewee. The adjusted response rate of this survey was 88% (3,166 out of 3,600 sampled respondents actually completed our questionnaire). About

23% (739) of the respondents (3,166) who participated in the survey were identified as the middle class according to the criteria explained in chapter 2.

The set of in-depth interviews was conducted with 223 residents in the three aforementioned cities in March and April 2008 (see Appendix). These interviewees were purposefully selected to represent various segments of the urban population, including middle-class individuals employed in both public and private sectors. To explore more nuanced explanations of the results from the probability-sample survey, the research team asked the interviewees to deliberate on several key issues that were also tackled in the probability-sample survey. On average, each interview lasted about two hours.

In both the probability-sample survey and the set of in-depth interviews, care was taken to minimize linguistic misinterpretations and respondent effects. The original content and wording of the questionnaire—which was first designed by this author in the United States—was reviewed by the researchers from the BASS to fit the Chinese social and cultural context and to provide for seamless translation from English to Chinese. College students of journalism and sociology, who had been trained by the project members in field interviewing techniques before the actual survey, were employed as field interviewers for both the probability-sample survey and in-depth interviews. Respondents in the survey and interviewees in the in-depth interviews were offered confidentiality and encouraged to provide answers that best captured their true feelings.

B. Generalizability of the Survey Data

Like all public opinion surveys that are adequately designed and executed, the three-city survey in this study produced two kinds of results: descriptive and relational.[14] Both kinds of results will be presented in this book. Both offer at least two profound *general* lessons for the study of the role of the middle class in democratization in China. First, although the *descriptive* results from the survey—such as those dealing with the extent of support for democratization and democracy itself among our respondents—cannot be directly applied to the entire country, they can certainly help to establish some needed statistical baselines against which the findings from other areas of the country can be compared. Furthermore, I assume that the general socioeconomic conditions may affect people's political attitudes. Consequently, the statistical baselines established in this study are especially relevant to and indicative of the middle class's political attitudes and behavior in urban areas at each of the *three economic development levels*, since the three cities in this survey were chosen to approximate these three levels.

Second, and more important, the findings from our three-city survey about the *relationships* among variables in this study can be directly generalized to other parts of China, especially among the middle class in urban China, since most, if not all, of these relationships are generic in nature.[15] These relationships in this study are mainly those (1) between the middle class's orientation toward democratization and its institutional and moral connections with the party-state and (2) between the middle class's democratic support and its political behavior. In fact, some recent empirical studies based on data collected from multiple-locale (as opposed to national) samples have generated insightful, generalizable inferences about the patterns of the relationships between sociopolitical variables in both urban and rural China.[16] When discussing the generalizability of the data from local samples (single and multiple locale) in the study of contemporary China, therefore, Melanie Manion (1994, 747) argues that "data from local samples can yield reliable answers, generalizable to a population beyond the sample, to a crucial category of questions—those about *relationships between variables*."

In short, while the descriptive results from our probability-sample survey may help establish the statistical baselines for the middle class's political attitudes and behavior in urban areas at three economic development levels, the relational results from the survey can be directly generalized beyond the three cities to explain various sociopolitical and socioeconomic correlates of such attitudes and behavior. Thus, it can be said that the data from this survey can have broad implications for our understanding of the level, causes, and behavioral consequences of democratic support within the middle class.

V. Précis of the Book

I begin my analysis with the definition, identification, and evolution of the middle class in China in chapter 2. In this chapter, I will first review and compare the two commonly used theoretical approaches to the definition of the middle classes: objective and subjective approaches. Between these two approaches, I determine which one is more suitable to our study of the new middle class in the unique socioeconomic context of contemporary China, a context that can be characterized by fast yet uneven economic development across regions. Based on the chosen theoretical approach, I identify the new middle class by specific occupations and shed some light on the size of the middle class in urban China. Having identified the middle class, I illuminate the role of the Chinese party-state in creating this social class and shaping its sociopolitical traits during such unprecedented, state-led socioeconomic transformations as the post-Mao reforms in contemporary China. All these analyses are intended to address three important questions: Who is the middle class by modern standards in contemporary China? What are the socioeconomic and sociopolitical statuses of the middle class compared to other classes? How has the party-state created and shaped this social class?

Chapter 3 is devoted to the examination of the extent of the middle class's support for democracy and its support for the CCP government. In the first part of the chapter, I explain how the empirical measures of support for democracy are designed, based on the results of various measures used in studies of both Chinese and non-Chinese settings. Using these measures designed for this study, I gauge the extent of our middle-class respondents' democratic support and, more important, compare it with that of the non-middle-class respondents' democratic support. Against this empirical evidence, I explore one of the propositions mentioned earlier: that is, compared to other classes, particularly the lower class who received less support from the party-state in post-Mao reforms, China's new middle class (especially those who are employed in the state apparatus) tends to be less supportive of any political changes toward democracy that may directly challenge the current party-state. Meanwhile, I investigate the potential variation of democratic support between two subgroups within the middle class: those employed in the state sector and those employed in the private sector.

In the second half of this chapter, I will examine the level of the middle class's support for the current government led by the CCP. It is assumed that the middle class's support for the government is closely related to its support for democracy and democratization. The measurement of support for the government in this study is systematically established based on the previous empirical studies of "political support" (see Easton 1965) in both Chinese and non-Chinese settings. Using this measurement, I estimate the strength of support for the current government led by the CCP among the middle-class respondents in the three-city survey, in comparison with that among the non-middle-class respondents. Based on the empirical findings of support for the government, I look into another proposition explained earlier in this chapter: that is, compared to the lower class, China's new middle class—especially those who are employed in the state apparatus—has stronger support for the current political regime led by the CCP. Furthermore, the correlation between support for the government and support for democracy among the middles-class respondents will be explored.

This chapter answers three questions in this study: Does the middle class in China support democracy and democratization?

Compared to other social classes, particularly the lower class, how strongly does the new middle class in China support democracy and the current party-state? Does the middle class's support for the party-state affect its support for democracy?

In chapter 4, I then examine the sociopolitical and sociodemographic sources of the middle class's democratic support. Following the contingent approach, which has been discussed earlier in this chapter, I hypothesize that the political orientation of the middle class in China may be shaped mainly by the middle class's connection with the state. To test the hypothesis, I explore two dimensions of this connection: institutional and ideational. The institutional dimension is measured by middle-class individuals' memberships with the Communist Party and their employment in the state sector, while the ideational connection is gauged by the beliefs of middle-class members in the values/norms promoted by the government led by the CCP. Meanwhile, I examine the effects of other key variables—such as sociodemographic attributes of the middle class and its perceived socioeconomic well-being—on this class's attitudes toward democracy. In this chapter, I seek to address one of the most critical questions that will enable us to better understand the role of the middle class in potential political changes in China: why does or does not the middle class support political changes toward a democracy in China?

The behavioral consequence of the middle class's democratic support is the analytical focus of chapter 5. The analysis of this issue is important because such behavioral consequences have *direct* implications for the future of the political system, as well as the sustainability of the current party-state in contemporary China. In this chapter, I first examine the forms and intensity of political participation by middle-class individuals in an urban setting. Then, I closely examine how the middle class's attitudes toward democracy variably influence each form of political participation and behavior. The findings about this issue will help us verify the last proposition, namely, that the low level of democratic support among the middle class tends to cause this class to act in favor of the current authoritarian state but in opposition to democratic change. This chapter is designed to address a crucial, practical question related to the behavioral consequences of the middle class's political attitudes: how do the middle class's attitudes toward democracy affect whether and how middle-class individuals participate in politics in this authoritarian, late-developing country?

Finally, in chapter 6, I highlight all major empirical findings from this study about the level, sources, and behavioral consequences of democratic support among the middle class. I then discuss crucial political implications from these findings for the role of middle class in democratization in China and important theoretical implications for such a role in the developing world.

China's Middle Class: Definition and Evolution

BEFORE ANALYZING THE political orientations of China's new middle class, I first need to conceptualize and identify this social class and describe its unique relationship with the party-state. Who are the middle class by modern standards in contemporary China? How has the party-state created and shaped this social class? What is the relationship between the middle class and the party-state? This chapter answers these specific questions. I begin with a review of the general approaches utilized to conceptualize and identify the middle class in the West, and then develop my own approach to the definition and operationalization of the middle class in China. Based on my definition and operationalization of the Chinese middle class, I will examine the evolution of the middle class, with emphasis on the middle class's interaction with the party-state.

I. Who Is the Middle Class in Contemporary China?

First of all, it should be noted that even in earlier studies of sociopolitical developments in the West and other parts of the world, the distinction was drawn between the middle class (the same or similar to the middle class defined in this study) and private entrepreneurs or capitalists. As will be discussed later, this distinction is made both "subjectively" (see, e.g., Centers 1949; Eulau 1956a, 1956b; Campbell et al. 1960; Lipset 1968; Hayes 1995; Walsh, Jennings, and Stoker 2004) and "objectively" (see, e.g., Alford 1962; Erikson and Goldthorpe 1992; Lipset 1968; Milbrath 1977; Nie, Powell, and Prewitt 1969; Verba and Nie 1972; Wright 1997). More important, as discussed later, these studies have also tried to discover the critical implications of such a distinction for the middle class's political attitudes and behavior.

To put this study of the Chinese middle class in the general theoretical framework and a cross-national context, I will here attempt to shed some light on the general theoretical approaches to the conceptualization of the middle class and their applications. These approaches mainly originated from the studies of the middle class in the West, as such a social class in the modern sense first emerged and thrived in the Western countries.

A. Subjective Versus Objective Approaches

In the conceptualization and operationalization of the middle class as a sociopolitical group, there are two distinct theoretical traditions in the studies of Western societies. One is the "subjective" approach (see, e.g., Centers 1949; Eulau 1956a, 1956b; Campbell et al. 1960; Lipset 1968; Hayes 1995; Walsh et al. 2004), and the other is the "objective" approach (see, e.g., Alford 1962; Erikson and Goldthorpe 1992; Lipset 1968; Milbrath 1977; Nie et al. 1969; Verba and Nie 1972; Wright 1997). The subjective approach suggests that, because a "social class is a psychological attachment that is part of an individual's overall self-concept" (Walsh et al. 2004, 470), the middle class is identified according to an individual's belief or perception that he or she belongs to the middle stratum of a certain society.

The origin of the subjective approach can be attributed to Aristotle. As Heinz Eulau (1956a, 236–237) summarizes,

[Aristotle] thought of classes as subjective rather than objective entities. Membership in a class, according to his way of thinking, is not determined by physical characteristics of any kind, such as wealth or income, or at least not definitely determined by such characteristics. Members of the middle class gain their position therein by thinking of themselves as above the lower class and below the upper class.

A modern forerunner of subjective class measurement, Richard Centers, emphasizes social classes as "psychological groupings, something that is essentially subjective in character, dependent upon class consciousness (i.e., a feeling of group membership), and class lines of cleavage [which] may or may not conform to what seem to social scientists to be logical lines of cleavage in the objective or stratification sense" (Centers 1949, 27).

According to this approach, importantly, such a psychological attachment to a social class significantly affects a person's political attitudes and behavior. For example, some empirical studies of the American public found that those who subjectively identified themselves with the middle class scored higher than did those who identified with the working class on measures of attitudes and behavior that were conducive to the maintenance of the democratic system in the United States (Eulau 1956a; Walsh et al. 2004).

On the other hand, the objective approach argues that a sociopolitical class is mainly determined by some key objective socioeconomic indicators, such as income, education, and occupation. Within this approach, there are two conceptual branches. One branch emphasizes the quantitative, cumulative property of the objective indicators (e.g., Nie et al. 1969; Verba and Nie 1972; Milbrath 1977; Sherkat and Blocker 1994). This branch, the "quantitative" branch, suggests that the best way to capture an individual's class identity is to form a quantitative index of income, education, and occupation and then to identify the person with a social class according to the person's position on the index. As a result, the middle class usually consists of those who are in the middle range of the scale. For example, Lester Milbrath (1977, 91) has suggested that "persons who scored high on all three factors would be placed in the upper class; those who scored high on two factors but medium or low on one factor would be in the next rank. Those who scored high on only one factor would be in the next rank, and so forth."

In a comparative study of five nations (the United States, Britain, West Germany, Italy, and Mexico), for instance, Norman Nie and his associates (1969) formed a weighted, quantitative index of objective indicators—including education, income, and occupation—and determined the middle class to be those who were in the middle third of the index. They found that, in the United States, about half of the population belonged to the middle class, while in the less developed Mexico, only 16% of the population fell in the middle class.

The other, "qualitative" branch of the objective approach stresses the qualitative properties of the various objective indicators of social class (e.g., Burris 1986; Erikson and Goldthorpe 1992; Glassman 1995; Wright 1997; Zipp 1986). This branch argues that the middle class is composed of those who possess a set of certain socioeconomic attributes, which qualitatively distinguishes the middle class from other social classes. As Martin Oppenheimer says (1985, 7), "class is not a quantitative measurement along some mathematical continuum, but a qualitative measurement representing groupings that are distinct and separate from one another."

Within the qualitative branch of the objective approach, the neo-Marxist measurement is the one most often used. The neo-Marxist measurement developed by Erik Olin Wright (1997) employs three subdimensions to form class categories: means of production, position in authority structure (based on managerial and supervisory responsibilities), and possession of skills and expertise. In the first subdimension, those having means of production are classified as owners; owners can be further divided into two categories: bourgeoisie and petite bourgeoisie, depending on the size of the means of production. In the second subdimension, those who supervise other workers are classified as managers. In the third subdimension, those possessing skills and expertise are classified as professional. The remaining society will be classified into working class, peasants, and unemployed. The middle class is defined as the petite bourgeoisie, managers, and professionals. More specifically, the petite bourgeoisie is referred to as the "old middle class," while managers and professionals are referred to as the "new middle class" (e.g., Burris 1986; Erikson and Goldthorpe 1992; Glassman 1995; Wright 1997; Poulantzas 1975).

B. An Alternative Approach to the Conceptualization and Identification of China's Middle Class

Objective Versus Subjective Approaches. In this study, I choose the objective approach over the subjective one for the identification of China's middle class. The main reason for this choice is that the unique social background of China's middle class seems to entail the objective approach for its conceptualization. Only beginning in the late 1980s was a middle class analogous to the Western middle class said to emerge gradually in China (Zheng and Li 2004; Xiao 2001; Lu 2004); moreover, as mentioned earlier, the class consciousness of the Chinese middle class is still in formation. The subjective approach requires most of the population to have at least a basic understanding of the middle class (vs. other classes, such as the working class and the upper class), an understanding that can take a long time to develop (Hayes 1995; Eulau 1956a, 1956b). According to Richard Centers (1949, 28–29), class consciousness "implies that a person's status and role with respect to the economic processes of society imposes upon him certain attitudes, values and interests relating to his role and status in the political and economic sphere. It holds, further, that the status and role of the individual in relation to the means of production and

exchange of goods and services gives rise in him to a consciousness of membership in some social class which shares those
attitudes, values and interests." In other words, class consciousness depends on "the extent to which members of the group are
aware of the reality of the group and of their own membership
in it" (Centers 1949, 75).

Do the Chinese people realize that they are members of a social
class, and if so, do they cognitively identify with their class? Chunling
Li (2003) suggests that many Chinese people still do not acknowledge the appropriateness of the concept of class in Chinese society,
and only a few of them have grasped the meaning of social class and
the criteria by which to identify different social classes. For example,
when asked to name some different social classes in Chinese society,
those in the less educated occupational groups could only identify
three groups: "rich people," "powerful people," and "ordinary people";
those in the well-educated occupational groups could identify some
groups in more specific terms, such as "government or party cadres," "private entrepreneurs," and "professionals." However, few of
the respondents identified the different social segments in terms of
"upper class," "middle class," and "lower class" (Chunling Li 2003).
As a result, the subjective approach, which relies mainly on the class
consciousness of the citizens, does *not* seem to be suitable for the
study of the newly emerged middle class in China.

*Quantitative Versus Qualitative Branches of the Objective
Approach.* Distinct from the subjective approach, the objective
approach relies only on objective indicators that are less likely to
be affected by the perception or misperception of class. Both the
quantitative and qualitative branches of the objective approach
have been applied to the identification of the middle class in some
early studies conducted in the Chinese setting. More important,
both branches argue that either quantitative or qualitative objective indicators of social class significantly influence people's beliefs
about politics.

Within the quantitative branch, a person's income has been considered the most common indicator of social class. For example,

David Goodman (1999) asserts that, as of 1997, in the more developed, coastal parts of South and East China, a person with a monthly income of above 5,000 to 6,000 RMB is considered a member of the middle class; in the less developed parts of West China, a person with a monthly income of above 3,500 to 4,500 RMB is regarded as a member of the middle class. Alastair Iain Johnston (2004) uses monthly household income to determine middle-class status. He says that "the middle class is constituted by respondents whose monthly household income is 3,000 RMB or more." Hangsheng Zheng and Lulu Li (2004) assert that, as of 2000, outside Beijing, an urban citizen with a monthly income of 1,000 to 10,000 RMB is a member of the middle class.

However, this income-based, quantitative measurement of middle class status has serious drawbacks in both practice and theory. First, it is very hard to achieve any consensus on the criterion of income when defining middle class, since *actual* personal income is hard to determine in today's China. There tends to be a huge gap between reported (or nominal) and actual incomes in China, because most income earners often kept their real incomes secret for various reasons, such as tax evasion (which is highly prevalent in China) (Shi 1997; Chen 2004). Moreover, in Chinese society, formal incomes (e.g., salary or wage) do not necessarily represent a person's real socioeconomic status. As Jie Chen points out (2004, 90): "most private entrepreneurs have much higher incomes than government bureaucrats. [However,] members of both groups may enjoy very similar living standards (in many cases, bureaucrats may enjoy even higher living standards than average private entrepreneurs).... While the entrepreneurs usually use their monetary resources to maintain such living standards, the bureaucrats in general achieve these standards through their administrative power and government perks."

Second, income varies dramatically among geographical areas in a fast-changing society such as China. For example, the average monthly income of residents in developed areas is 2.5 times higher than the average of those in underdeveloped areas. And the average monthly income of urban residents in China is 2.5 times higher than the average of those in rural China. Moreover, the average monthly income of urban residents in developed areas is 5.4 times higher than the average of rural residents in underdeveloped areas (Chunling Li 2003). Thus, it becomes problematic to use one set of income criteria to stratify social classes.

To offset these disadvantages of the quantitative branch of the objective approach, the qualitative branch of the objective approach has offered some alternatives more suitable to the socioeconomic conditions of contemporary China. Among the studies informed by this qualitative branch, Xueyi Lu and his associates (2002, 2004) map out the most comprehensive structure of social stratification in China. Drawing upon the neo-Marxist measurement,[1] Lu and his associates utilize four dimensions—means of production, position in authority structure, possession of skills and expertise, and position within or outside the government system (*tizhinei* or *tizhiwai*)—to classify social groups or classes. It should be noted that of these four dimensions, position within or outside the government system is unique to the Chinese sociopolitical setting. They argue that, unlike Western societies, the state or government has exerted a tremendous impact on the pattern of social stratification in Chinese society. In China, those positioned in the core of the government system usually enjoy many more sociopolitical and economic privileges than those positioned outside the political system. As I have discussed, for example, government bureaucrats may not earn more income than private entrepreneurs, but they nonetheless have higher living standards by virtue of their administrative power. Lu and his associates, therefore, have distinguished three positions in the government system in China today: the core of the government system, the periphery of the government system, and outside the system. The core of the government system includes most government agencies (*zhengfu bumen*) within the party and state apparatus and some advantaged public organizations (*shiye danwei*), which are non-profit organizations in the public domain. The core of the government system monopolizes the power of redistributive benefits and enjoys a large portion of redistributive benefits. The periphery of the government system includes disadvantaged public organizations and enterprises owned by the central government or local governments (*guoyou qiye*). The periphery of the political system has little redistributive power, enjoys only a small portion of redistributive benefits, and has had to extract resources from their market activities. Most collective enterprises (*jiti qiye*), private enterprises, foreign-related enterprises, self-employed businesses, and peasants are positioned outside of the political system and thus enjoy few redistributive benefits.

Within this unique sociopolitical context, Lu Xueyi and his associates (2002, 2004) identified ten social strata by occupation in contemporary Chinese society: (1) administrative personnel of state affairs and social affairs, (2) managerial personnel, (3) private entrepreneurs, (4) professionals, (5) office workers (*banshi renyuan*), (6) self-employed individuals (*ge'ti'hu*), (7) service workers, (8) industry workers, (9) peasants, and (10) unemployed and semi-unemployed. Table 2.1 shows the positions of each social stratum in the four dimensions: means of production, position in authority structure, possession of skills and expertise, and position in the political system.

According to Xueyi Lu and his associates, administrative personnel of state affairs and social affairs, such as bureaucrats in government agencies, are positioned in the core of the government system, monopolize the political resources, and enjoy most of the redistributive benefits.[2] Private entrepreneurs are those owners of enterprises that employ more than eight non-family employees and that were legitimized as a part of the Chinese economy only after 1988. Private entrepreneurs own the large means of production. While they were positioned outside the government system, entrepreneurs were gradually co-opted by the party-state (Dickson 2003).

Managerial personnel include all mangers in state-owned, private, and joint venture enterprises. They do not own the means of

Table 2.1 A Model of Social Stratification in China

	Position in Labor Division	Position in Authority Structure	Means of Production	Inside/Outside the Political System (*tizhinei/tizhiwai*)	Major Resources
Administrative personnel of state affairs and social affairs	High- and middle-level professional and technical rank	High- and middle-level management	Agents (do not possess means of production, but control or dispose)	The core of the political system	Political
Managerial personnel	High- and middle-level professional and technical rank	High- and middle-level management	Employees (do not possess means of production, but control or dispose)	The periphery of the political system or outside the system	Cultural or political
Private entrepreneurs	High- and middle-level professional and technical rank	High-level management	Employers (possess means of production)	Outside the political system	Economic
Professionals	High- and middle-level professional and technical rank	Self-managed or managed (independent to some extent)	Employees or self-employed (do not possess means of production)	Inside the political system or outside the system	Cultural
Office workers (banshi renyuan)	Middle- and low-level professional and technical rank	Managed or middle- and low-level management	Employees (do not possess means of production)	Inside the political system or outside the system	Some cultural and political

Self-employed labors (ge'ti'hu)	—	Management or self-managed	Self-employed or employers (possess means of production)	Outside the political system	Some economic
Commercial and service workers	Skilled, semiskilled, and unskilled labors	Managed or low-level management	Employees or self-employed (do not possess means of production)	Inside the political system or outside the system	Some cultural or political
Industrial workers	Skilled, semiskilled, and unskilled labors	Managed or low-level management	Employees or self-employed (do not possess means of production)	Inside the political system or outside the system	Some cultural or political
Peasants	Skilled, semiskilled, and unskilled labors	Self-managed	Employees or self-employed (possess some means of production)	Inside the political system or outside the system	Some economic or cultural
Unemployed	—	—	—	—	None

Source: The content of this table is drawn from Lu (2002, 2004).

production; rather, they have the responsibility of managing the means of production. Most of them are well educated and possess some "cultural capital" (specialized training and skills).

Professionals are those with occupations that involve specialized training and skills, and they include engineers, accountants, lawyers, doctors, university professors, researchers, and so on. Since the professional occupations require specialized training and skills, most professionals possess cultural capital.

Office workers (*banshi renyuan*) include staff members in the government and party agencies and office workers in all types of enterprises and organizations. They hold white-collar jobs and most of them have at least a university-level education.

The self-employed individuals (*ge'ti'hu*) are those owners of businesses that employ fewer than eight non-family employees. They own some means of production and manage their businesses themselves. Unlike the private entrepreneurs who own a large amount of economic capital, most self-employed individuals own only a small amount of capital. In the Chinese context, most self-employed individuals are not well-educated, especially those who started their businesses in the 1980s.

In the lower socioeconomic standings are service and industrial workers, peasants, and unemployed persons. Service workers are those who work in the wholesale or retail trade or other service-related occupations. Industrial workers include those in all types of production-related enterprises. Usually, China scholars combine service workers and industrial workers into one category as "workers."[3]

Peasants are agricultural workers who live in rural China.[4] Generally, peasants possess no means of production and are not in a position to access the benefits distributed by government among urban residents. Unemployed and semi-unemployed refer to those who do not have a job at all or who do not have a stable occupation.

Qualitative Branch of the Objective Approach as an Analytical Framework. As mentioned earlier, this book draws upon the qualitative (as opposed to quantitative) branch of the objective approach to identify China's middle class. This branch of the objective approach overcomes the drawback that the quantitative branch has suffered. This is mainly because, in contemporary China, occupations are much easier to determine and are more consistent across regions than personal income, and they tend to represent "groupings that are distinct and separate from one another" (Oppenheimer 1985, 7). Therefore, the occupation-based, qualitative measurement (of the objective approach) should be a more reliable and useful indicator of the middle class in the Chinese setting than the income-based, quantitative measurement. In addition, the qualitative measurement seems to be more promising for cross-national comparison, since the modern occupations used in this measurement (i.e., white-collar professional, private entrepreneur, managerial personnel, and white-collar office workers) arise largely from the general trends of modernization and industrialization at the global level, and hence have commonalities across countries (see, e.g., Marsh and Kaase 1979).

Consequently, based on the conceptualization of the qualitative branch within the objective approach, I collapse the ten social strata—developed by Lu and his associates (presented in Table 2.1)—into three social classes: upper class, middle class, and lower class. The upper class includes administrative personnel of state affairs and social affairs, as well as private entrepreneurs. The lower class is then identified with self-employed individuals (ge'ti'hu), service workers, industry workers, peasants, and the unemployed and semi-unemployed. Finally, I operationalize the middle class in urban China by combining three major social strata typically used in both Chinese and non-Chinese settings:[5] managerial personnel, professionals, and office workers (banshi renyuan) (Table 2.2). In China, this new middle class has gradually emerged since the early 1980s when the post-Mao economic reforms were initiated by the party-state.

Based on the survey of the urban population in the three cities, Beijing, Chengdu, and Xi'an, I have found as follows (see Table 2.3).

First, the results from Table 2.3 show that 2.5%, 24.4%, and 73.0% of our respondents belonged to three objectively conceptualized social classes, respectively: the upper class, middle class, and lower class.[6] Second, the results also indicate that the Chinese social structure is still pyramid shaped: the smallest social class is an upper class

Table 2.2 Definition and Operationalization of the Middle Class in China

	Occupations
Managers	The managers of state-owned, collectively owned, and privately owned enterprises; the managers of foreign and joint venture enterprises
Professionals	Research, educational, and medical specialists (e.g., scientists, professors, teachers, and doctors); engineers, technicians, and their assistants; economic and legal professionals (e.g., accountants, lawyers, and so on), cultural/art and sports professionals; creative intellectuals (e.g., writers, musicians, and consultants); all other kinds of self-employed professionals
White-collar office workers	The staff members in the government and party agencies; the office workers and staff members in public organizations and all types of enterprises

Table 2.3 Distribution of Social Classes in the Three Cities: Beijing, Xi'an, and Chengdu

Objective Class Identity	**% (*N*)**
Upper class	2.5 (80)
Middle class	24.4 (773)
Lower class	73.0 (2313)
Total	100 (3166)

that occupies the apex of Chinese society; the second smallest class is the middle class that has not become the dominant social class in urban China; the largest social class is a vast population of the lower class that lies at the bottom of Chinese society.

II. The Emergence and Evolution of the New Middle Class

The last half-century has witnessed the dominant role of the state institutions in shifting the patterns of social stratification in Chinese society. In this process, how has the relationship between the state and the newly emerged middle class been shaped since the outset of the post-Mao reform? The answers to this question will help us understand the origins of the new middle class's orientation toward democracy and democratization.

A. Market Transition Versus State-Centric Models

There are two major analytical models used in the studies of the Chinese new middle class's evolution and its relationship with the state: the market transition and the state-centric models. The market transition model argues that in the past several decades of the post-Mao reform, the emerging market forces have gradually diminished the state's influence in social stratification through the introduction of new mechanisms of resource allocation and the alteration of the opportunity structure that used to be monopolized by the party-state (Parish and Michelson 1996; Nee 1989; Zhou, Tuma, and Moen 1996). According to this model, the state and market represent two fundamentally different systems of resource allocation. The rise of the market in the post-Mao era has created alternative sources of rewards not controlled by the state institutions, and such a shift reduces individuals' dependence on the state (Nee 1989, 1991, 1996; Nee and Matthews 1996). Moreover, this model suggests that as power—that is, control over resources—shifts progressively from the state to market, there is a change in the distribution of social values favoring those who hold "market power" rather than state or administrative power (Nee 1989, 1991, 1996).[7] As the market economy grows in post-Mao China, the Chinese middle class will gain market power and hence become more independent politically.

By contrast, the state-centric model emphasizes the continued influence of the party-state on ordinary citizens' lives during the reform era (Bian and Logan 1996; Rona-Tas 1994; Zhou 2000; Zhou et al. 1996). The premise of the state-centric model is based on a conviction that the state plays a crucial role in setting up institutional contexts within which social forces interact. According to this model, the Chinese state has enjoyed strong capacities to penetrate society in general and to guide economic transformations in particular. This is because this state has two unique, powerful ruling pillars: the dominance of the single, Leninist party and the prerogative of the government to intervene in any socioeconomic sphere (Walder 1995a). Thus, the state-centric model suggests that "given the historical role of the state in China..., there is no reason to doubt that the remaking of institutional rules in China's economic transformations will be heavily influenced by...the state's own interests" (Zhou 2000, 1141). Through its policies and decrees implemented in the post-Mao reforms, the Chinese state has created and molded a new middle class in both the private and public sectors. Due to the dominant role of the state in influencing the career and life opportunities of the newly rising middle class, this social class has become very dependent upon the party-state. As David G. Goodman (1999, 260–261) points out, the Chinese middle class, in general, is "far from being alienated from the party-state or seeking their own political voice, and appears to be operating in close proximity and through close cooperation" with the party-state.

Of these two analytical models, the state-centric one seems to be more suitable for our understanding of the new Chinese middle class's evolution and its relationship with the state. The state-centric model correctly puts the party-state in the center of the post-Mao socioeconomic transformations, which have brought about the new middle class in China. Therefore, this model can help us better comprehend why, despite the societal transformations wrought by market forces in post-Mao China, the state has continued to play an important role in determining the overall patterns of social stratification and facilitating the emergence of the new social strata such as the middle class (see, e.g., Parish and Michelson 1996).

To better understand the unique and critical role that the Chinese state has played in shaping the middle class, I examine the evolution of this social class since the establishment of the Chinese Communist Party (CCP)-led People's Republic of China in 1949. It is hoped that by examining the evolution of the middle class, I can offer some historical evidence to support an argument that this social class is dependent upon the party-state.

B. Historical Background: The Middle Class Before 1949

The pre-1949 Chinese society may be divided into urban and rural sectors. The rural social structure was characterized by the dominance of a small number of gentry and landowners over the large number of landless peasants. On the other hand, the urban social structure was seen as the dominance of a small number of upper-class bourgeoisie and comprador capitalists over a large number of urban proletariat. Two dominant social phenomena should be noted here. One is that over 80% of the Chinese population lived in the rural areas and less than 20% lived in the cities. The other phenomenon is that, with economic development and the gradual industrialization in the first part of the twentieth century, the middle class in China[8] at that time emerged mainly in the cities.

In this kind of general social structure, the Chinese middle class of that time constituted only 3% of the population right before 1949.[9] This small but gradually rising middle class had gained some economic and/or political independence under the rule of the Nationalist Party[10] and had a greater degree of self-determination in regard to such matters as their life style and occupational advancement, much like their counterparts in Western societies (Davis 2000).

C. The "Quasi-Middle Class" in the Mao Era

With the establishment of the People's Republic of China (PRC) in 1949, the new Communist government, following the orthodox Marxist ideology, committed itself to the elimination of class differences to create a classless and equal society. The direct consequence of this commitment was the so-called destratification, in which the observed class lines of the pre-1949 era were eliminated (Parish 1984). First, to achieve the destratification of social classes, the Communist Party took measures to eliminate the economic bases of private economy. In the rural areas, the party used the land reform to confiscate most of the wealth and land of the landlord class and redistribute them to the landless peasant class. In the urban areas, by the early 1950s, the party had nationalized all large enterprises owned by the bureaucratic and comprador capitalists who had close ties with the Nationalist Party or foreign capital. Over time, most of these enterprises evolved into state-owned enterprises under the direct administration of the central government. In addition, the government in the 1950s launched a program of collectivization of the industrial and commercial enterprises owned by the petite bourgeoisie—the so-called handicraft industrialists (*shou gongye zhe*).

The result of the land reform campaign in the rural regions and the socialization of industry and commerce in the urban areas was that the basis of the private economy was eliminated. Almost no Chinese citizens *owned* private assets (e.g., land, living quarters, capital, or business firms). To permeate and institutionalize this profound social change, the PRC's 1954 Constitution did not recognize the existence of private property. Nor did it protect such property.[11] Eventually, by 1958, the economic foundations of class differentiation were almost completely eliminated from Chinese society.

Second, the party-state took measures to control occupational mobility in urban China. Almost all urban citizens were assigned to various types of work units (*danwei*).[12] In general, there were four major types of work units: (1) government and party agencies (*dangzheng jiguan*), (2) public organizations (*shiye danwei*), (3) state-owned enterprises (SOEs) (*guoyou qiye*), and (4) collective enterprises (*jiti qiye*) (Wu 2002; Zhou 2004). The work units not only fulfilled administrative or production responsibilities but also assumed important social responsibilities, including that of providing employees with housing, education, medical care, and other public goods (Tang and Parish 2000; Shi 1997). Thus, in the cities during the Mao era, it was almost impossible for anyone to survive without being associated with a work unit, because almost all basic services were available only through the work unit rather than the market (Wu and Treiman 2004).

The direct result of the work unit system in the cities was that people from all walks of life became "work unit dependent." Through this system, the party-state controlled the occupational mobility of urban residents. It was the party-state that assigned every citizen to the various work units. Moreover, many of these assignments tended to be fixed for life. For example, under the work-unit control of labor, "only half the workers could change jobs in a lifetime or 1%–2% per year" (Bian 2002, 93).

Moreover, the occupational advancement was determined by the CCP and government. Life chances under the Maoist regime were, according to many studies, primarily determined by one's exhibited or presumed political loyalties to the CCP (Cao 2001; Walder 1989, 1995a). In addition, "political criteria are systematically incorporated and enforced in the allocation of opportunities for higher education, better jobs, and more power and privilege" (Cao 2001, 687). According to Susan Shirk (1984, 59), the emphasis on political loyalties "contributes to the processes of *political consoli-dation*." The system of reward for political loyalties is much more amenable to political control than is a system of reward for merit. And the definition of political loyalty is very broad, which allows the CCP elites to exploit it to promote their loyal supporters.

As a result of these Maoist policies, the pre-1949 middle class ceased to exist. In its place, however, "a stratum of the salaried civil servants [or workers]" (Davis 2000, 272) emerged. This social stratum only somewhat resembled the pre-1949 middle class or a middle class by Western standards to the extent that some of the professions in this stratum were similar to, if not the same as, those in a typical middle class in the West. For lack of a better term for this unique social group, let us call this social stratum the "quasi-middle class." It should be noted that there were several structural aspects to this transformation. First, the land reform campaign in the rural region and the nationalization of industry and commerce in the urban region eliminated the private economy. Thus, the economic foundations—such as private properties—of the middle class were almost completely destroyed.

Second, the party-state controlled the occupational mobility of urban employees through the system of work units, assigning managers and professionals to various positions and determining their occupational advancement based on their political loyalties. Additionally, immediately after 1949, the CCP adopted the system of unified job assignment (*tongyi fenpei*) for college graduates. Under this system, all the jobs of graduates were assigned by the government based mainly on their political correctness. As a result, college graduates lost their autonomy in regard to employment. Thus, the backbone of the post-1949 quasi-middle class—managers and professionals—became "fundamentally dependent on the Party-state in every sphere of life" (Davis 2000, 271).

Third, the party launched a series of political campaigns to strengthen its political control over the quasi-middle class. The 1957 Anti-Rightist Campaign persecuted more than 500,000 managers and professionals for being "rightists," and most of these "rightists"

were sent to rural China to be "reeducated." In the political campaigns that followed, these rightist households suffered systematic
discrimination. The persecution of the intellectuals and professionals, who were the core of the quasi-middle class, culminated in the
Cultural Revolution. In addition, many professionals and managers were "pulled down" from their places and "replaced with new
cadres (workers, peasants, and soldiers) who lacked the education,
professional training, and know-how to manage the specific tasks
at hand" (Lin and Xie 1988, 797). All these campaigns and policies
made the quasi-middle class politically vulnerable and psychologi-
cally unconfident.

Finally, the homogenization of consumption patterns and life
styles in the Mao era eliminated the distinct life style of the middle
class in Chinese society (Davis 2000; Whyte 1975). This homogenization of consumption patterns and life styles was primarily
caused by two factors. One is that the rationing system, used in
the state-controlled distribution of consumption items, housing,
and other social services, could not form the basis for widely differ-
ing consumption patterns (Whyte 1975). The other factor is that
the distinct middle-class consumption patterns and life styles were
harshly criticized by the CCP. For example, during the Cultural
Revolution, a middle-class life style was considered as a key indicator of class enemies. For this reason, well-educated professionals and managers were careful to adopt, to the extent possible, the
life style of the working class. This need to repress the distinct life
styles and cultural consumptions that the pre-1949 Nationalist
Party had left relatively unrestricted meant that "the professional
and managerial stratum lost important resources with which to
define and reproduce themselves socially" (Davis 2000, 271).

D. The Emergence of the New Middle Class in the Post-Mao Era

The post-Mao reform era (1978–present) represented a significant
departure from the Mao era (1949–1978) and witnessed a profound

change in the patterns of social stratification in Chinese society dramatically. While Maoist China was characterized by the social "destratification," post-Mao China has seen the gradual return of the pre-1949 social stratification. Since 1978, Chinese society has become increasingly differentiated and stratified. This profound change in social structure has been caused by major policy initiatives of the post-Mao party-state since the outset of the reforms.

Economic Privatization. The CCP has gradually legitimized the existence and nurtured the growth of the private sector in post-Mao China (Zheng 2004a). The development of private economy in China has experienced three major stages of economic privatization, each of which was initiated and guided by the party-state. The first stage (1978–1983) is marked by the official revival of private business. However, in this stage the CCP only officially recognized the "individual" (or small-scale) businesses (*ge'ti'hu*).[13] For example, Article 11 of the 1982 Chinese Constitution states that "the individual economy of urban and rural working people, operated within the limits prescribed by law, is a complement to the socialist public economy." Originally, the sector of individual businesses was "intended to play a marginal, stopgap role and to act as a 'supplement' to the state and collective sectors, 'filling the gaps' they left in the economy, particularly in the distribution of consumer goods and services and in employment" (International Finance Corporation 2000, 8).

The second stage of privatization (1984–1992) is characterized by the rise of the "private enterprises" (*siying qiye*),[14] which are distinguished from the individual businesses to the extent that private enterprises may have more employees. According to the revised Article 11 of the 1988 PRC's constitution, private enterprise is allowed to hire more than the previously permitted eight non-family employees. This constitutional provision officially recognized the existence and growth of private enterprises (Chen 1995; International Finance Corporation 2000).[15] As the new Article 11 states, "the government allows the private economy to exist and develop within the limits prescribed by law." Accordingly, in June 1988, the State Council issued the "Tentative Stipulations on Private Enterprises" to govern the activities of private firms.

The third stage of economic privatization (1993–present) was commenced by Deng Xiaoping during his famous southern tour in September 1992. In this southern tour, Deng Xiaoping called for a continued reform of China's economy and determined China's future transition to a market economy. At the Fourteenth CCP Congress in 1992, the socialist *market* economy was first officially endorsed as China's goal of reform (International Finance Corporation 2000). At the same time, the party-state even encouraged its officials to engage in activities of the private economy or "plunge into the sea of commerce" (*xiahai*). In 1992, party cadres and government officials were the second-largest group in the private sector, but by the mid-1990s they had become the largest group among private entrepreneurs (Zheng 2004b). As a result, the social statuses of private entrepreneurs and individual businesses were significantly elevated in Chinese society. All these changes and individual wealth generated from the private sector attracted more Chinese citizens to become involved in the private sector.

In September 1997, the Fifteenth CCP Congress recognized the non-state economy as an important component of the "socialist economy." In March 1999, the National People's Congress revised the 1982 Chinese Constitution and legalized the status of the non-state economy and private ownership. The reform of SOEs since 1995 accelerated the pace of economic privatization. In 1995, the central government formulated a policy—"keep the large ones and let the smaller ones go" (*zhuada fangxiao*)—to reform SOEs. This policy resulted in massive privatization of most small and medium state-owned enterprises or collective enterprises (Dittmer and Gore 2001).

As a consequence of the state-led privatization, private entrepreneurs and self-employed individual businesses expanded rapidly in the 1990s and became the greatest beneficiary of the Dengist reform (Dickson 2003; Pearson 1997). Table 2.4 indicates that the gross industrial output from the state-owned enterprises declined from 55% in 1990 to 27% in 1998, while that from individually owned enterprises increased from 5% to 16% during the same period. Moreover, the other types of enterprises, comprising private enterprises and joint venture enterprises, increased to 22%.

Social Mobility. Before the post-Mao reforms, Chinese urban residents were assigned by the state to certain work units, and they were hardly allowed to move among work units in their lifetime. With the deepening of post-Mao reforms, Chinese citizens gradually obtained the discretion to determine their own employment.

After the early 1980s when the post-Mao reforms started, the CCP took a series of steps to restructure the state apparatus to suit market-oriented economic reforms, and these steps have inevitably reduced the scope of state involvement in individual lives (Pearson 1997; Dittmer and Gore 2001; Dickson 2003). One of the most profound steps taken by the central government was

Table 2.4 Gross Industrial Output by Types of Enterprises in China, 1980–1998

Year	State-Owned Enterprises (%)	Collective-Owned Enterprises (%)	Individually Owned Enterprises (%)	Other Types of Enterprises (%)	Total (%)
1980	76.0	23.5	0	0.5	100
1985	64.9	32.1	1.9	1.2	100
1990	54.6	35.6	5.4	4.4	100
1991	56.2	33.0	4.8	6.0	100
1992	51.5	35.1	5.8	7.6	100
1993	47.0	34.0	8.0	11.1	100
1994	37.3	37.7	10.1	14.8	100
1995	34.0	36.6	12.9	16.6	100
1996	33.7	36.5	14.4	15.4	100
1997	29.8	35.9	16.9	17.4	100
1998	26.5	36.0	16.0	21.5	100

Source: The data in this table are drawn from Zheng (2004a, 66).

to reorganize and overhaul SOEs. Since the early 1980s, the CCP has taken measures to reform SOEs and gradually granted SOEs greater autonomy. In the beginning, the government intended to invigorate SOEs by giving a proportion of fiscal autonomy to the enterprises (Chen 1995). In 1987, the government introduced the contract responsibility system (CRS). According to the CRS, "SOEs were contracted to pay income tax and adjustment tax on a specific level of profit. If they exceeded the contracted level of profit, they were taxed at a lower rate on their additional profit.... The CRS aimed to improve enterprise performance by strengthening financial responsibility, emphasizing profitability, and giving enterprises greater autonomy in decision-making" (Zheng 2004a, 111).

In the late 1980s and early 1990s, based on the principle of "separation of ownership from operating rights" (Chen 1995, 56), the central government granted SOE managers more autonomy to manage their enterprises. For example, in 1992, all SOE chief managers were given freedom to hire and fire employees "without consulting a municipal labor plan or obtaining the approval of their own governmental superiors as had been general practice since the late 1950s" (Davis 1999, 28). Meanwhile, after 1990, the government also gradually stripped SOE workers of their privileges such as lifetime employment, subsidized housing, low-cost medical care, and guaranteed pensions (Dittmer and Gore 2001).

In September 1992, the Chinese government announced a new policy that allowed all employees to "move at their own discretion between state, private and collective enterprises." This policy signified "a clear blow to the administrative barriers that had previously obstructed [job mobility]" (Davis 1999, 28–29). As a result, ordinary Chinese citizens had greater freedom to choose where they worked and what they did for employment. As Deborah Davis (1999, 34) observed, for example, "between January 1990 and July 1995, 41 per cent [of Shanghai residents] had changed employer at least once; 5 per cent [of them] had changed three or more times. Moreover, in most cases switching employers simultaneously involved changing to a different line of work, a pattern that stands in clear contrast with past practice where many people spent an entire career with one employer."

The new policy has also resulted in more opportunities for occupational advancement among ordinary people. Since 1978, more and more Chinese citizens have improved their occupational status by moving to the private sector, such as by running their own businesses or working in private, foreign, and joint venture enterprises. Because of the need to promote economic modernization, the party-state has also modified its criteria for recruitment and promotion within the state apparatus. Specifically, the government has gradually de-emphasized the importance of political loyalties to determine one's upward advancement (Cao 2001; Parish and Michelson 1996; Walder 1995a; Walder, Li, and Treiman 2000). Consequently, "many new middle-level and high-level cadres are professionals because recruitment in the state bureaucracy now favors university degree holders, professional training, and other forms of human capital" (So 2003, 371).

Generally speaking, because of the market-oriented reforms in the post-Mao era, the value and prestige of certain occupations have changed and ordinary people have gained more opportunities for career mobility (Davis 1992a, 1992b; Lin and Xie 1988). There is a clear trend toward assigning higher value and prestige to those professional and managerial positions commanding knowledge and education. The status hierarchy that places white-collar work above blue-collar work has been established: the managerial-professional personnel are better paid than the blue-collar workers, and the former live a life style that resembles the middle class's life style in the developed world.

Parenthetically, it is worth noting why the middle class in contemporary China is considered a *new* middle class. In the Mao era, the middle class was gradually eradicated by the party-state from Chinese society during a series of political campaigns and movements. The middle class in contemporary China, which is the focus of this book, emerged in the post-Mao era. First of all, because of its young age, this middle class is considered "new" or "first generation of middle class" (Zhou 2002), unlike its counterpart in the West that has existed for more than two hundred years, during which many middle-class families have experienced intergenerational successions.

Second, in terms of composition and social origins of the middle class in contemporary China, this social class can also be considered new, because it is distinct from the traditional middle classes that have evolved in the West. The evolution of the middle class in Western societies has experienced three stages, and its composition has changed accordingly. During the period of capitalist revolution (from the seventeenth to eighteenth centuries), free farmers, artisans, and urban bourgeoisie constituted the main components of the middle class in Western societies (Glassman 1995, 1997). With economic development, early trade capitalism was replaced by industrial capitalism, and the composition of the middle class changed accordingly. Starting from industrial capitalism in the late nineteenth and early twentieth centuries, "a moderately prosperous middle class of small business people and shopkeepers replaced the artisans as the middle class of the industrial-capitalist system" (Glassman 1995, 158). During this period, small businessmen, merchant farmers, and some professionals constituted the majority of the middle class. Since World War II, high-tech industrial capitalism has replaced industrial capitalism, and a new type of middle class has emerged to become the backbone of the middle class: technocrats, professionals, managers, bureaucrats, and white-collar office workers (Kahl 1957; Mills 1953; Poulantzas 1975), and the old-fashioned middle class of industrial capitalism (i.e., small businessmen and merchant farmers) dramatically shrank in the composition of the middle class.

However, in China, free farmers or merchant farmers never became an important part of the new middle class. More important, since the beginning of the post-Mao reform, the old-fashioned middle class (i.e., self-employed laborers) and the new middle class (i.e., managerial personnel, professionals, and civil servants) emerged at almost the same time. Thus, when I use the term "new" to describe the middle class in contemporary China, I really mean that this middle class is the first generation in contemporary Chinese society, and its composition is distinct.

E. Major Components of the New Middle Class

Overall, the post-Mao reform changed the social structure and consequently paved the way for the emergence of a new middle class, which is identical to its counterparts in other industrialized, market economies. As defined earlier in this chapter, China's new middle class includes mainly three occupational groups: managerial personnel, professionals, and office workers (*banshi renyuan*).

First, the managerial stratum has been the most important component of the new middle class, in terms of its social stature and its role in the rising market economies in urban China (Bian 2002; Lu 2002, 2004; Zheng and Li 2004; Qiu 2004). There are three subgroups of the managerial stratum. The first is composed of managers of SOEs and collective enterprises, who used to be the government-appointed administrators of these enterprises before the post-Mao reform. The second subgroup includes the managers of private enterprises. The third subgroup consists of the managers of foreign-related enterprises or the so-called *sanzi qiye* (i.e., equity joint venture, contractual joint venture, and solely foreign-owned enterprises). According to the estimate offered by Xueyi Lu and his associates (2010), in 2004, the managerial stratum accounted for around 1.5% of the population.

Second, the professional stratum includes those occupations that involve specialized training and skills. This mainly includes scientific researchers, all kinds of technicians and personnel of scientific and technical work and their assistants, financial and legal professionals (e.g., accountants and lawyers), teachers and professors, and cultural and sports workers. This stratum is characterized by the possession of human capital (e.g., specialized skills and knowledge). According to a recent nationwide survey (Lu 2010), the professional stratum accounted for around 5.1% of the nation's population in 2004.

Finally, the group of office workers (*banshi renyuan*) mainly includes two subgroups. One includes office workers and staff members in public organizations and in all types of industrial enterprises. The other subgroup is composed of staff members in government and party agencies (*gongwuyuan*) whose ranks are lower than department director (*chuji*) in the central government or provincial governments and whose ranks are lower than section director (*keji*) in local government (Zhang 2005). According to the most recent national survey conducted by the Chinese Academy of Social Sciences (Lu 2010), the *banshi renyuan* group constituted around 4.8% of the population in 2004.

F. The Two-Track Formation of the New Middle Class

It should be noted that in general, both the state institutions and market institutions play a critical role in the formation of different social classes. As Figure 2.1 clearly indicates, those people

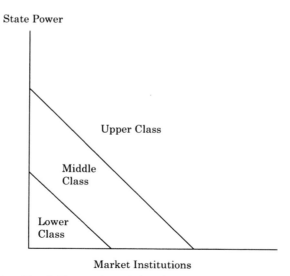

FIGURE 2.1 The Two-Track Formation of the New Middle Class.

who sit at the top of the hierarchy of both state institutions and market institutions form the upper class, which mainly included administrative personnel of state affairs[16] and social affairs and private entrepreneurs.[17] This all-powerful hybrid, known as a "cadre-capitalist" class, has "monopolized political capital, economic capital, and social/network capital in the Chinese society," and its members are "the beneficiaries of the existing arrangements of partial reforms, mixed economy, and hybrid ownership" (So 2003, 369). In other words, this upper class has almost unlimited political, economic, and social power in Chinese society. On the contrary, those people who are at the bottom of the hierarchy of both state institutions and market institutions form the lower class, which enjoys the least political, economic, and social leverage in society. It is in the middle of the hierarchy that the middle class resides. Consequently, the middle class possesses limited political, economic, and social power, which is more than the power at the disposal of the upper class but less than that of the lower class.

According to this framework, the formation of the middle class in contemporary China follows two distinct paths. One is through the state institutions: people become members of the new middle class through their employment in various positions within the state sector. These people are mainly managers in state-owned enterprises, professionals in public organizations, and staff members in government and party agencies and public organizations. The access to such positions is considered "closed,"[18] that is, subject to state screening for political loyalty and/or party membership (Walder et al. 2000). The political values and well-being of this subgroup of the new middle class has inevitably been heavily affected by the state.

The other path of the formation of the new middle class is through market institutions: people become members of the middle class through their occupations in the non-state sector. The access to these occupations is considered "open," because it is determined more or less by the workings of the market institutions with state intervention. As suggested by Victor Nee and Rebecca Matthews: "the shift to markets opens up alternative sources of rewards not controlled by the redistributive state, and this shift thereby reduces dependence on the state" (Nee and Matthews 1996, 408). Thus, this subgroup of the middle class employed in the non-state sector, which includes the managers in the private and foreign-related enterprises, professionals in the non-state sector, self-employed laborers, and white-collar office workers in the non-state entities, is less dependent than the other subgroup on the state. Nonetheless, it should immediately be noted that compared to the lower class, this subgroup of the middle class is more appreciative of the state since it has been one of the largest beneficiaries of the state-led economic development.

In the representative sample of our three-city survey conducted in 2007–2008, about 60% of the middle-class respondents belonged to the state sector subgroup (those employed in the state sector), whereas about 40% of them fit in the non-state-sector subgroup (those employed in the non-state sector).

G. The Growth of the New Middle Class

Since the advent of the post-Mao reform, four factors have contributed to the emergence and rapid growth of China's middle class: the expansion of college education, the development of the private economy, the inflow of foreign direct investment (FDI), and the reform of enterprises and public organizations. More important, the effects of these factors have been decisively enhanced and channeled by the reformist policies of the party-state.

First, as discussed earlier, since 1978 the government has legalized the private economy and made efforts to encourage its development, and thus, the private sector has reemerged and grown rapidly in Chinese society. The expansion of the private sector has helped create a large number of the middle-class jobs, such as the positions of managerial personnel and professionals.

Second, education is the essential accelerator of the formation of the middle class. Since 1978, the state has made continuous and genuine efforts in strengthening and expanding higher education nationwide, from reopening the universities in the early period of reform to increasing government budgets for higher education in the following years. These efforts have resulted in a rapid expansion of the social base of the new middle class (Lu 2002, 2004; So 2003; Zhang 2005). Table 2.5 illustrates that from 1978 to

Table 2.5 The Enrollment of Students in Four-Year Colleges and Universities: 1978–2004

Year	Yearly Enrollment (in 10,000)	Total Enrollment (in 10,000)	Yearly Graduate (in 10,000)
1978	40.2	85.6	16.5
1980	28.1	114.4	14.7
1985	61.9	170.3	31.6
1986	57.2	188.0	39.3
1987	61.7	195.9	53.2
1988	67.0	206.6	55.3
1989	59.7	208.2	57.6
1990	60.9	206.3	61.4
1991	62.0	204.4	61.4
1992	75.4	218.4	60.4
1993	92.4	253.6	57.1
1994	90.0	279.9	63.7
1995	92.6	290.6	80.5
1996	96.6	302.1	83.9
1997	100.0	317.4	82.9
1998	108.4	340.9	83.0
1999	159.7	413.4	84.8
2000	220.6	556.1	95.0
2001	268.3	719.1	103.6
2002	320.5	903.4	133.7
2003	382.5	1108.6	187.7

Source: The data in this table are drawn from Zhang (2005, 305–306).

2004, the number of students enrolled in colleges and universities grew rapidly. For instance, the total enrollment in higher education nearly tripled from 1999 to 2003. College graduates in turn formed the backbone of the managerial and professional strata in the new middle class. In addition, the old system of "centralized job assignments" (tonyi fenpei) of college graduates by the government was gradually phased out; graduates became autonomous in job seeking and career pursuit. By 1993, for instance, "70 per cent of that year's graduates had found employment on their own" (Davis 1999, 30). The liberalization of the job market for college graduates undoubtedly enhanced their career mobility, which in turn contributed to the growth of the middle class.

Third, the inflow of foreign capital helped create more middle-class job positions in China. After 1978 the FDI flow into China soared. For example, in the first two decades of post-Mao reform, from 1979 to 1999, China pulled in over $306 billion in utilized FDI, second only to the United States worldwide (Gallagher 2002, 346). The post-Mao leadership began to open China's door to foreign investment in the 1970s by initiating special economic zones (SEZs) (i.e., Shenzhen, Zhuhai, Shantou, and Xiamen), in which "foreign investment was encouraged by lower tax rates, fewer and simplified administrative and customs procedures, and, most crucially, duty-free import of components and supplies" (Naughton 2007, 406). By 2003, the central government had established six SEZs, fifty-four national-level economic and technological development zones (ETDZs), and fifty-three new and high-tech industrial development zones, all of which adopted preferential policies to attract foreign capital. The inflow of foreign capital has created numerous middle-class (or white-collar) jobs. For example, the first group of Western-style professional managers emerged with the introduction of foreign capital in post-Mao China, a group that has been one of the major components of China's managerial stratum.

Finally, the state-led reforms of SOEs, collectively-owned enterprises, and government institutions also facilitated the emergence

Table 2.6 The Distribution of Party Members in Ten Social Strata in Four Cities, 1999

	Shenzhen	Hefei	Hanchuan	Zhenning
Administrative personnel of state affairs and social affairs	100.0	77.5	100.0	100.0
Managerial personnel	35.7	58.8	53.8	—
Private entrepreneurs	22.2	24.4	9.1	0.0
Professionals	27.2	25.2	17.8	24.0
Office workers (banshi renyuan)	28.2	40.7	54.5	46.3
Self-employed laborers (ge'ti'hu)	13.7	10.4	7.7	5.2
Service workers	10.4	7.6	10.6	3.9
Industrial workers	0.0	13.3	5.9	10.3
Peasants	—	—	4.3	5.2
Unemployed and semi-unemployed	2.0	9.1	1.8	3.9

Source: The data in this table are drawn from Lu (2002, 35–36).

and growth of the middle class. The reforms of state-owned and collective enterprises turned their managers into white-collar professionals, a part of the newly emerged middle class (Goodman 1999; Zheng and Li, 2004; So 2003). This group of managers is the biggest component of China's managerial stratum, and they took advantage of the post-Mao reform in SOEs to gain tremendous personal wealth and prominent social status (Goodman 1999). Furthermore, due to the party-led reform of government institutions for the purpose of promoting economic development, government agencies at various levels have put more emphasis on merit and specialized skills in recruitment and promotion. Such a change has certainly transformed old positions of party-state workers into the new positions of white-collar professionals in these institutions, although the latter still owe their employment to the state (Zhang 2005; Lam and Perry 2001).

H. Institutional Incorporation

The post-Mao party-state has also adopted a set of institutional arrangements to incorporate this class into the state's socioeconomic and political orbit. These institutional arrangements can best be characterized as "state corporatism."[19] Since the early 1980s, as Margaret Pearson (1997) points out, these corporatist arrangements have had a profound impact on the relations between the party-state and the newly emerged social classes, such as the new middle class and private entrepreneurs. As a result, the middle class was not only created but also shaped by the party-state.

Specifically, the post-Mao state has adopted two key institutional measures to mold the relations between the middle class and the state. The first institutional measure has been to recruit the newly emerged middle class into the CCP. In 1999, for example, a majority of the party members in four Chinese cities, Shenzhen, Hefei, Hanchuan, and Zhenning, were from the newly emerged middle class (Lu 2002, 36). As Table 2.6 indicates, except the political elites (i.e., administrative personnel of state and social affairs), the middle class (including managers, professionals, and office workers) had the highest percentage of party membership. In comparison, the lower class (including the workers and peasants who were considered "leading classes" in the Mao era) ranked the lowest in party membership. These trends show that the party-state has put more efforts into co-opting the newly emerged social classes, such as the middle class and private entrepreneurs, through the party organization. The middle class's party membership clearly signifies its close relationship with the party-state, since the latter still uses the party organization to control and mobilize social groups and to strengthen its political ties with these groups.

The party has made relentless efforts to use organizations other than the CCP to link the state with the new middle class. These organizations include government-sponsored trade unions, state-sanctioned religious organizations or churches, government-sponsored professional and academic organizations, and government-sponsored sports and recreation associations. These organizations have a dualist nature. On the one hand, they are licensed by the state and are supposed to disseminate state directives and to their members. On the other hand, the organizations, at least in theory, are charged with expressing the interests of their members to the state.

The data from our three-city survey indicated that middle-class people were more likely to participate in these kinds of organizations run by the state than were lower-class people. Approximately 47.3% of middle-class people indicated that they participated in at least one of the nine corporatist organizations included in the survey,[20] while 23.6% of the lower-class people participated in at least one of these organizations. These findings suggest that the newly emerged middle class has been incorporated by the current regime through a set of corporatist organizations.

III. Summary and Conclusion: Sociopolitical Traits of the Middle Class

In this chapter, I have tried to answer two critical questions: Who are the members of the middle class in today's China? And what is the role of the party-state in creating and shaping this class? Based on the qualitative branch of the objective approach, I have operationalized the middle class in China by combining three occupational groups: managerial personnel, professionals, and office workers (*banshi renyuan*). The results from the three-city survey show that within the urban population in

Beijing, Chengdu, and Xi'an, about 24.4% belonged to the objectively conceptualized middle class.

Unlike the middle class in the West, the development of China's middle class was heavily influenced by the state. Given the preponderant role that the party-state has played in the post-Mao socioeconomic transformation, the newly emerged middle class has been created and shaped by the state, and hence is considered to be closely associated with the state. As this chapter has shown, the state has adopted a set of policies, such as the legitimization of private economy, the reform of state-owned and collective enterprises, and the restructuring of party-state agencies, which have nurtured an environment for the development of the new middle class in the post-Mao era. Meanwhile, the state also adopted a set of institutional measures, such as recruitment of middle-class individuals into the party and the restructuring of corporatist organizations, which have strengthened the political ties between the middle class and the state. All in all, it is expected that the ties between the party-state and the middle class, formed during the emergence and expansion of this social class, should have a profound impact on the middle class's attitudinal and behavioral orientations toward democracy and democratization. This proposed impact will be examined in the chapters that follow.

3

How Does the Middle Class View Democracy and the Chinese Communist Party Government?

THE PREVIOUS CHAPTER depicted the vital role of the party-state in the emergence and expansion of China's new middle class in the post-Mao era. That chapter also implied that the bond that the middle class had enjoyed with the party-state and the benefits that this social class had received from the state after the post-Mao reforms would influence the middle class's orientation toward democracy and democratization. In this chapter, I will examine the levels of the middle class's support for democracy, as well as its support for the Chinese Communist Party (CCP) and its government. This chapter attempts to answer three central and closely related questions: Relative to the lower class, how much does the middle class support democratic values and institutions in post-Mao China? And compared to the lower class, how much does the new middle class support the current CCP government? Finally, does the middle class's support for the CCP government affect its support for democracy and democratization in China?

Among scholars of the middle class and democratization, as mentioned at the outset of this book, there seems to be no clear consensus on these questions. Furthermore, almost none of the early studies on these issues were based on systematic probability samples[1] of middle-class individuals, samples that could provide robust and conclusive findings about the levels of the middle class's support for democracy, as well as its support for the government in China. To help fill this gap, this chapter uses data collected from a probability-sample survey conducted in three Chinese cities in late 2007 and early 2008 to determine the levels of the middle class's support for democracy and for the government and to explore the relationship between these two kinds of support. To achieve this goal, in this chapter, I first operationalize and gauge the middle class's support for democracy and for the CCP government, and then I explore the correlation between the two kinds of support. Finally, I discuss the theoretical and political implications of the empirical findings.

I. The Middle Class's Views on Democracy

Drawing on studies of both Chinese and non-Chinese settings (e.g., Almond and Verba 1963; Dahl 1971; Huntington 1991; Gibson 1995; Chen and Zhong 2000), I operationalize support for democracy as positive attitudes toward a set of democratic norms and institutions. The democratic supporter, according to James Gibson's (1995, 55–56) synthesis of writings on democratic support, is "the one who believes in individual liberty and who is politically tolerant, who holds a certain amount of distrust of political authority but at the same time is trustful of fellow citizens, who is obedient but nonetheless willing to assert rights against the state, who views the state as constrained by legality, and who supports basic democratic institutions and processes." In this study, I measure this kind of support among our respondents by tapping into their attitudes toward three democratic norms—rights consciousness, political liberty, and popular participation—and one fundamental democratic institution, the popular and competitive election of political leaders. While these norms and institutions do not exhaust all the democratic principles, they do serve as the core of democracy and hence as a good test of democratic support among our respondents.

Furthermore, in the analysis that follows, I will compare democratic support in the middle class and non-middle class.[2] While this study focuses on the middle class's democratic support, such a comparison may help us gauge the level of the middle class's support in China's contemporary sociopolitical context.

A. Rights Consciousness

Rights consciousness is the degree to which citizens are aware of and willing to assert individual rights for themselves. According to Gibson, Duch, and Tedin (1992, 343), "to the extent that citizens are vigilant about their rights, democracy tends to flourish." Moreover, in China, belief in individual rights is an especially important and sensitive indicator of democratic values, since China's traditional culture is said to work against this democratic norm. According to Chinese traditional culture, individuals should not be in a position to claim their own rights, because this culture emphasizes collective (or group) interests and government authority over individual rights (e.g., Pye 1992).

To detect the strength of rights consciousness within the middle class relative to that among the non-middle class, I asked our respondents to indicate whether a series of rights ought always to be protected or whether protection depends on the circumstances. The responses of the Chinese middle class are shown in Table 3.1 alongside those of the non-middle-class urban residents.

Like the non-middle-class respondents, over 90% of middle-class respondents believed that such individual rights as the rights to work, to education, to free access to public information, to privacy of personal correspondence, and to travel abroad should always be protected. Moreover, over 80% of our respondents thought that such individual rights as the rights to reside

Table 3.1 Rights Consciousness

	Supportive Response by the Middle Class (%)	Supportive Response by the Non-middle Class (%)
Right to work	94.0	93.6
Right to education and training	94.6	94.5
Free access to public information	93.1	94.2
Right to privacy of personal correspondence, telephone conversations, and so on	93.2	94.2
Right to travel abroad	91.1	90.2
Right to reside anywhere in the country	81.9	82.9
Religious liberty and freedom of conscience	85.9	85.8

Note: Entries are the percentage of respondents asserting that the right ought to always be respected. Approximate *N*s of the middle-class respondents are 739, whereas the *N*s of non-middle-class respondents (excluding private entrepreneurs or capitalists and ranking government officials) are 2,330.

anywhere in the country and to worship freely ought to be protected. These findings suggest that like the non-middle class, the members of the Chinese middle class are very eager to protect their own individual rights.

B. Valuation of Political Liberty (Versus Order)

There are at least two distinct propositions on the valuation of political freedom by the citizens in transitional societies, such as the former Soviet Union and the People's Republic of China (PRC). On the one hand, a group of scholars who studied such valuation in the former Soviet Union (Gibson et al. 1992, 341) assume that "democracies require citizenries committed to liberty even when there is a prospect for disorder." When designing instruments to measure the level of mass support for democracy in the former Soviet Union, therefore, they hypothesize that respondents who support democracy as a set of political institutions and principles would choose liberty over order. Moreover, Gibson and his associates suggest that even within a political culture (i.e., the Soviet political culture) that has a "penchant for order" (Gibson 1995, 80), democratic supporters would be more likely to choose liberty over order (see Gibson et al. 1992; Gibson and Duch 1993; Gibson 1995). In short, their theoretical approach seems to suggest that the preference for political liberty over order is almost unconditionally, positively related to support for democratic institutions and principles.

On the other hand, emphasizing the uniqueness of Chinese political culture, some China analysts suggest that the Chinese conceptualize and prioritize certain democratic principles quite differently than their counterparts in some other societies, especially the West (e.g., Nathan 1990, 1997; Scalapino 1998). Specifically, in terms of the relationship between social order and democracy, as Nathan (1997, 204) has pointed out, Chinese political culture tends to assumes that "democracy should be conducive to social harmony [or order]." Moreover, Chinese political culture emphasizes social order and collective interests over individual rights and liberty. As Pye (1992, 123) has pointed out, most Chinese "accept completely the need for order." Some empirical findings from earlier survey studies of urban China also support this proposition (Chen and Zhong 2000). In addition to the cultural factor, material interests could also prompt the Chinese middle class to favor social order over democratization or democracy. This is because these interests—such as professional mobility, employment stability, and ownership of private property—could be harmed by social disorder in a society where the majority of the population remains in the social strata below the middle classes. As a China scholar (Xiao 2003, 62) points out, the Chinese middle class might resist democracy if its members perceived that democratic change would cause social upheavals and hence harm their self-interests.

Table 3.2 Valuation of Political Liberty (Versus Order)

	Supportive Response by the Middle Class (%)	Supportive Response by the Non-middle Class (%)
In general, demonstrations should not be allowed because they frequently become disorderly and disruptive. (Disagree)	22.9	35.6*
The harmony of the community will be disrupted if people form their organizations outside the government. (Disagree)	23.5	37.4*

Note: The nature of the "pro-political liberty" response to these items is shown in the parentheses. Approximate Ns of the middle-class respondents are 739, whereas the Ns of non-middle-class respondents (excluding private entrepreneurs or capitalists and ranking government officials) are 2,330.
* Difference between the responses by the middle class and by the non-middle class is significant at the .05 level.

To explore these two propositions, I fashioned questions that assumed a conflict between political freedom and social order. Table 3.2 reports the responses of the Chinese middle class, along with those of lower-class people, in three cities.

Overall, the evidence in this table shows that the support for political freedom among the Chinese middle class is not very strong in either absolute or relative terms. Only about 23% of the middle-class respondents supported the idea that a public demonstration as an expression of political freedom should be allowed even though it could turn disorderly and disruptive, whereas about 36% of non-middle class respondents were in favor of this idea. Similarly, only 24% of middle-class respondents thought that citizens should be able to form their own organizations outside the government even if the harmony of the community were disrupted,[3] while a higher percentage (37%) of non-middle-class people shared such a thought. These findings suggest that, even though the Chinese middle class has become vigilant about its own rights, it still favors social order over political freedom. These findings apparently support one of the two propositions mentioned earlier: that is, when political freedom is pitted against potential social disorder, the Chinese middle class decisively chooses the latter.

C. Support for a Participatory Norm

Another important democratic value is popular participation (see Almond and Verba 1963). As many democracy scholars point out, democracy is a system wherein the people of a society control the government. In a democratic society, political power originates from the people living in this society and is delegated by the people to the government (Dahl 1971; Locke 1967; Macridis 1992, chapter 2). Thus, those who support democracy should be willing to participate in politics to exercise such popular power. In China, support for the participatory norm is an extremely critical indicator of democratic values, because there is said to be no tradition in China of popular influence on the government. It has been suggested that the political culture of China is rooted in Confucianism, which emphasizes deference to authority and grants a sage the "mandate of heaven" to rule the country (Pye 1992).

In this survey, I include two items to measure support for this participatory norm. One relates to citizens' participation in government decision making in general; the other relates to their role in initiating major political change. The frequency distribution of the two items is reported in Table 3.3.

The results clearly indicate that support for the participatory norm was quite weak among the middle-class respondents in both absolute and relative senses. Only one-fourth of middle-class respondents (25%) were in favor of participation in the government decision-making process, and less than one-third (28%) of them believed that ordinary people should have any role in initiating political reform. On the other hand, non-middle-class respondents scored

Table 3.3 Support for Participatory Norm

	Supportive Response by the Middle Class (%)	Supportive Response by the Non-middle Class (%)
Government leaders are like the head of a family; I should always follow their decisions and don't need to participate in government decision making. (Disagree)	24.9	33.7*
Measures to promote political reform should be initiated by the party and government, not by ordinary people (*laobaixing*) like me. (Disagree)	28.1	40.1*

Note: The nature of the "pro-participatory norm" response to these items is shown in the parentheses. Approximate *N*s of the middle-class respondents are 739, whereas the *N*s of non-middle-class respondents (excluding private entrepreneurs or capitalists and ranking government officials) are 2,330.
* Difference between the responses by the middle class and by the non-middle class is significant at the .05 level.

higher than middle-class respondents on both questions (see Table 3.3). These findings suggest that the Chinese middle class does not seem to be supportive of this participatory norm, which is considered one of the most important democratic principles.

D. Support for Competitive Election

Most scholars of democracy consider competitive, multiple candidate elections among independent political organizations imperative for a functioning democratic system (e.g., Schumpeter 1947; Dahl 1971; Huntington 1991). They believe that only through such an institutionalized process can a government be established that is based on popular sovereignty and that serves the common good. As Schumpeter (1947, 269) points out, democracy is an "institutional arrangement for arriving at political decisions in which individuals acquire the power to decide by means of a competitive struggle for the people's vote." Therefore, a belief in competitive elections has been considered an essential component of democratic values, which democratic supporters must acquire in a transition from a non-democratic regime to a democratic system (Gibson et al. 1992).

The support for competitive elections is of particular interest in Chinese society. This is because the *fully* competitive election (i.e., multicandidate *and* multiparty election) of government leaders has not happened in mainland China since 1949. Furthermore, as some China analysts (Chen and Zhong 1998, 32) point out, "it is...relevant to tap into the level of support for competitive elections in China, since Chinese political culture has been deemed inherently non-democratic."

To measure support for competitive elections, I employed two items in the three-city survey. One refers to the multicandidate election of government leaders at various levels (*geji*) in general, while the other relates to competition among political parties in elections. The results from the two items are reported in Table 3.4.

About the same percentage (70%) of respondents in both the middle class and non-middle class supported multiple-candidate elections for government leaders. But respondents from the middle class had a lower level (25%) of support for multiparty competition in such elections than did those from the non-middle class (39%). These findings from the two items together apparently suggest that most of the middle-class respondents support competitive, multiple-candidate elections for leaders with the condition that such elections are not "among several parties." Since in reality the CCP has always dominated and controlled elections at almost all levels and several so-called democratic parties have served at best consultative roles in politics, rejection of multiparty competition in elections seems to imply a consent to the current one-party-dominance election system (with the multiple-candidate competition within this system).

Table 3.4 Support for Competitive Election

	Supportive Response by the Middle Class (%)	Supportive Response by the Non-middle Class (%)
Government officials at various levels should be selected by multiple-candidate elections. (Agree)	69.9	71.2
Competition among several parties in election of government leaders should not be allowed. (Disagree)	24.9	38.7*

Note: The nature of the "pro-competitive election" response to these items is shown in the parentheses. Approximate Ns of the middle-class respondents are 739, whereas the Ns of non-middle-class respondents (excluding private entrepreneurs or capitalists and ranking government officials) are 2,330.
* Difference between the responses by the middle class and by the non-middle class is significant at the .05 level.

E. The Interrelatedness of Democratic Subdimensions

Thus far, it has been implicitly argued that these four sets of attitudes toward democratic values and institutions are part of a more general belief system. It is expected that the scales created among these sets are themselves interrelated. To explore this expectation, I ran a factor analysis of these four sets of attitudes among both middle-class and non-middle-class respondents. The results from the factor analysis show that only a single dominant factor emerged among these four sets, accounting for 45.6% of the original variance (Figure 3.1).[4] Three of the four sets load strongly on this factor, and the remaining set has a moderate loading. The set of questions about support for participatory norms has the highest loading. The sets for valuation of political freedom and support for competitive elections also contribute substantially to the factor of democratic support.

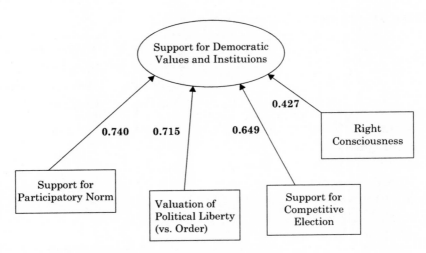

FIGURE 3.1 Interrelatedness of Democratic Subdimensions

The set of questions on rights consciousness has only moderate loading. A possible explanation for this moderate loading could be that the results of this set of questions lacked variance: as reported earlier, almost 90% of our respondents in our sample believed that the series of individual rights listed in the questionnaire ought to be always respected and protected.[5]

Based on these findings from the factor analysis, one may conclude that there is a reasonable amount of coherence among the attitudes of our respondents toward these sets of democratic values and institutions. In other words, those who tend to support one democratic value tend also to support other democratic values. Given this degree of coherence among these dimensions of democratic support among both middle-class and non-middle-class respondents, the factor score from this factor analysis will be used as the collective indicator of democratic support in the multivariate analyses that follow.

F. Summary

How supportive is the middle class in urban China of basic democratic values and institutions? The answer to this question according to our analysis is twofold. On the one hand, like most of the lower class people, most members of the Chinese middle class are vigilant about the individual rights that are closely related to their own interests. On the other hand, however, most members of this class are not willing to claim their political rights (such as engaging in public demonstration and forming their own organizations) if such rights could *possibly* disrupt social order; they are not disposed to have a say in government affairs and to play a role in initiating a political change; they seem to support competitive elections only within the current one-party-dominated and -controlled electoral system. From a comparative perspective, it has also been found that the middle class as a whole is even less supportive of democratic principles and institutions in these areas than is the lower class.[6]

Overall, while this new middle class likes to have its individual rights protected, it does not seem to be eager to support and participate in political change toward a democratic system. The findings seem to support the arguments from some earlier studies of the middle class in contemporary China that while the middle class may "expect a system of checks and balances that could effectively constrain party power" (Chen 2002, 416) from infringing on their own economic and social interests, they are not ready to support and participate in political changes favoring democracy (Goodman 1999; Chen 2002; Xiao 2003; Zheng and Li 2004; Zhang 2005). In addition, these findings echo some early observations of the middle classes in the Pacific Asian region in the mid-1990s. For example, in Singapore, the majority of the middle class accepted the undemocratic government as long as the authoritarian regime continued to satisfy their material needs (Lam 1999; Rodan 1996). In Malaysia, the burgeoning middle class, especially ethnic Malays, either actively supported an increasingly authoritarian state or remained politically apathetic (Bell 1998; Jones 1998; Torii 2003). In Indonesia, the new middle class stood firmly on the side of the status quo (Bell 1998; Jones 1998). Even though Taiwan and South Korea became successful democracies, the role of the middle class in supporting democratization were questioned in a few studies. These studies suggested that in both South Korea and Taiwan, the new middle classes did little to stimulate democracy, and their class interests were tied to the developmental state (Brown and Jones 1995; Jones 1998).

The characteristics of the middle class's attitudes toward democratic values and institutions—which are revealed by the data from the probability-sample survey of the three cities—can also be substantiated and further illuminated by the results from my in-depth interviews of many middle-class people. For instance, consider this case as follows.

Mr. 94 worked in the bureau of finance in a municipal government for more than fifteen years in the city of Xi'an.[7] At the time of the interview he was serving as the director of the inspection department within the bureau. The interview with Mr. 94 took place in a trendy coffee shop. At the beginning, we talked about his family; he was quite proud of his son, since he went to a very prestigious university in Beijing. After a few moments of casual talk to break the ice, I asked him to tell me his view of democracy and democratization in China. He said:

Western democracy is not suitable for China because it lacks social infrastructure. The present system fits China very well. First, the advantage of the current system is that it can use the centralized power to respond to large-scale disasters quickly and maintain order effectively. For example, in the Sichuan earthquake, our government played an effective role in making sure all the supplies were quickly delivered to the earthquake areas and social order was restored. Moreover, because people [in the lower class] do not understand the democratic political system very well, democracy will cause disorder and chaos in society. What we need to do is to improve our own "socialist democracy"; we should not just copy the West. Democracy is a good thing but it needs centralization first. To some extent, electoral democracy or "all-people" democracy will negatively impact current economic development; so we need democratic centralism, which means party-led, systematic consultation among the masses.

II. The Middle Class's Views on the Chinese Communist Party Government

In addition to my findings, presented previously, about the level of the middle class's support for democracy, I have thus far suggested that the new middle class in China does not seem to support democracy, mainly because its members are connected with and appreciative of the current authoritarian state. Before I test in the next chapter this relationship between the middle class's support for democracy and its support for the state, I now closely examine the level of the middle class's support for the state itself, particularly relative to the lower class. My examination will enable a more nuanced understanding of the main causes of the middle class's democratic support.

There are at least three different views in the recent literature regarding the middle class's general attitudes toward the current CCP government. One view suggests that the new middle class is very supportive of the government, because most of middle-class members "enjoy a comfortable life style and a high socioeconomic status relative to other groups" in the post-Mao state-led development (Wright 2010, 83). Another view argues that the new middle class has not formed any consistent attitudes toward the government, since this social class not long ago emerged from different sociopolitical backgrounds, each of which has a separate kind of influence on the varied sectors of the middle class's political attitudes (e.g., Liang 2011, 260). Finally, some of the most recent analyses have at least implied that most members of the new middle class have become increasingly critical of the current CCP government, because many policies of the government—which are aimed solely at the growth of GDP—have hurt some fundamental interests of the middle class, such as education for children and urban housing (e.g., Yang 2011; Zheng 2011).

Among the aforementioned observations of the middle class's general attitudes toward the current CCP government, none was based on representative, probability-sample surveys of that social group. Based on the data collected from my probability-sample survey of the three cities, I seek to evaluate these three competing views.

A. Definition of Support for the Government

My measurement of support for the government (or political support) within the middle class and the non-middle class is designed based on the theoretical framework developed by David Easton (see Easton 1965, 1976). Easton's definition of political support begins as follows: "We can say that A supports B either when A acts on behalf of B or when he orients himself favorably toward B. B may be a person or a group; it may be a goal, idea, or institution. We shall designate supportive *actions* as overt support and supportive *attitudes* or sentiments as covert support" (Easton 1965, 159). The "covert support" is referred to as support for the government or political support in this study.

According to Easton, political support consists of two dimensions—"diffuse support" and "specific support" (see Easton 1965, 1976). Diffuse support, often seen as the more influential dimension, represents a person's support for the regime with regard to the fundamental values, norms, and institutions of the government. It is believed that citizens are linked to the regime by diffuse support based on their assessment of the fundamental values, norms, and institutions of the government. Thus, diffuse support for the regime is also regarded as the "belief in legitimacy" of the political regime (Easton 1965, chapter 18). According to this conceptualization, specifically, diffuse support in this study refers to the middle class's supportive attitudes toward the fundamental values that the current, post-Mao regime advocates and the basic political institutions through which the regime rules the country.

The other dimension of political support, specific support, means a person's satisfaction with specific policies and performance of the incumbent government. Easton (1976, 437) suggests that this dimension of support is "object-specific": "people are or can become aware of the political authorities—those who are responsible for the day-to-day actions taken in the name of a political system." Citizens are linked to the political authorities through their specific support derived from their perceptions and evaluations of the actual policy outputs of the authorities. Based on this conceptualization, specific support here denotes the middle class's positive assessment of public policies made by China's incumbent central authorities in dealing with major socioeconomic issues (e.g., inflation, housing, job security, employment, social order, corruption, etc.).

B. Measurement of the Two Dimensions of Political Support

To operationalize the concept of diffuse support for the political regime or regime legitimacy, many scholars have identified several major aspects of the concept. For Lipset (1981), regime legitimacy is tied to affect for the prevalent political institutions in a society. David Easton (1965, 1976) sees regime legitimacy (or "diffuse support" in his original term) as an affect *primarily* for values, norms, and institutions of the regime. Combining these two approaches, Muller and Jukam (1977, 1566) identify three major operational components of the concept of regime legitimacy: (1) "affect tied to evaluation of how well political institutions conform to a person's sense of what is right"; (2) "affect tied to evaluation of how well the system of government upholds basic political values in which a person believes"; and (3) "affect tied to evaluation of how well the authorities conform to a person's sense of what is right and proper behavior [or conduct]." Following Muller and Jukam's operationalization of regime legitimacy,[8] some China analysts (e.g., Chen 2004; Chen and Dickson 2010) have designed and tested several specific survey instruments to gauge the level of regime support among the general population and the private entrepreneurs in contemporary China. Based on the results of these instruments from the earlier studies, I fashioned seven items (or statements) to detect the levels of diffuse support for China's current political regime among the middle-class and non-middle-class respondents in my survey, as follows:

1. I believe that the party represents my interests.
2. I respect the political system in China today.
3. I believe that the people's congress represents and serves the people's interests.
4. I believe that People's Liberation Army can protect our nation.
5. I believe that the police enforce the laws impartially.
6. I believe that the judiciary administers justice impartially.
7. I believe that my personal values are the same as those advocated by the government.

Specifically, items 1 through 6 are together designed to gauge a respondent's evaluations of the political authorities and major political institutions in terms of whether the authorities have functioned and wielded their power in accordance with one's sense of fairness and basic interests. Item 7 is intended to measure the affect for the values/norms that the current CCP regime has promoted. Respondents were asked to assess each of these seven statements on a five-point scale, where "1" stands for strong disagreement with the statement and "5" refers to strong agreement with it. These seven items were combined to form an additive index of a respondent's support for the current CCP regime.[9]

The results of these seven items are presented in Table 3.5. Two important findings can be discerned from the results. First, one can find from this table that the middle-class respondents in our survey scored higher than the non-middle-class respondents for

Table 3.5 Distribution of Diffuse Support

	Positive Response (%)[c]		Mean		Standard Deviation	
	Middle Class	Non-middle Class	Middle Class	Non-middle Class	Middle Class	Non-middle Class
1. I believe that the party represents my interests. (1–5)[a]	82.8	79.1	4.21	3.86	.826	.81
2. I respect the political system in China today. (1–5)[a]	85.7	81.1	4.44	4.04	.74	.74
3. I believe that the people's congress represents and serves the people's interests. (1–5)[a]	84.2	80.0	4.17	3.91	.77	.74
4. I believe that PLA can protect our nation. (1–5)[a]	83.6	82.1	4.15	4.10	.69	.66
5. I believe that the police enforce the laws impartially. (1–5)[a]	65.0	60.4	3.78	3.61	1.00	.99
6. I believe that the judiciary administers justice impartially. (1–5)[a]	62.5	58.5	3.72	3.55	1.00	.99
7. I believe that my personal values are the same as those advocated by the government. (1–5)[a]	79.3	75.5	4.03	3.71	.76	.77
Entire index (7–35)[b]	—	—	27.6	27.9	4.03	3.88

[a] "1" to "5" are the numerical scores assigned to each item of the regime support: 1 = strongly disagree, 2 = disagree, 3 = just so-so, 4 = agree, and 5 = strongly agree.

[b] This additive index is constructed by combining all seven items to capture a collective profile of a respondent's regime support, ranging from 7 (indicating the lowest level of regime support) to 35 (indicating the highest level of regime support).

[c] The percentage of positive responses is the combination of the percentage of those who either "agree" or "strongly agree" with the questionnaire statement.

all seven items (which collectively measure diffuse support for the political regime). Specifically, the percentage of the middle-class respondents who either agreed or strongly agreed with each of the seven statements was higher than that of the non-middle-class respondents who did so. This finding was also reinforced by the results of the mean scores presented in Table 3.5: the mean score of each of the seven items among the middle-class respondents was higher than that among the non-middle-class respondents. Furthermore, as the same table shows, the mean score of the diffuse support *index* for the middle-class respondents was also higher than that for the non-middle class.

The other important finding from the results presented in Table 3.5 is that although the middle-class and non-middle-class respondents' assessments of all seven statements in the diffuse support index were quite positive, there were quite noticeable variations among their assessments. Specifically, both the middle-class and non-middle-class respondents gave the highest scores for the item regarding one's respect for the current political system in China (item 2), while they all gave the lowest scores for the items about the police and the court (items 5 and 6). This finding was substantiated by the percentages of all respondents who registered positive responses to these items (i.e., items 2, 5, and 6) and the mean scores of the respondents' assessments of these three items.

In sum, the results presented in Table 3.5 have revealed that (1) the middle class seems to be more supportive of the fundamental values, norms, and institutions of the CCP government than non-middle-class people, and (2) both groups expressed the most positive feeling about the fundamental political system in China.

To operationalize the other dimension of political support, specific support for the incumbent CCP authorities, I asked the respondents to assess the authorities' performance in ten policy areas: controlling inflation, providing job security, minimizing inequality, improving housing, maintaining order, providing medical care, levying taxes, providing social welfare, combating pollution, and fighting corruption. The results of my presurvey test of the survey questions and the results from other studies (Chen 2004; Chen and Dickson 2010) have proved that all ten policy areas are critical to most people in contemporary China, including those in the middle class and those in the non-middle class. Based on these results, I designed ten questionnaire items to measure our respondents' evaluation of the authorities' performance in ten policy areas, as follows:

1.   Controlling inflation
2.   Providing job security
3.   Minimizing inequality
4.   Improving housing
5.   Maintaining order
6.   Providing medical care
7.   Levying taxes
8.   Providing social welfare
9.   Combating pollution
10. Fighting corruption

For each of the items listed, respondents were asked to "grade" government policy performance based on the grading scheme commonly used in China's schools: on a 1 to 5 scale, where 1 = very poor, 2 = poor, 3 = so-so, 4 = good, and 5 = very good. These ten items were combined to form an additive index of a respondent's specific support for the incumbent CCP authorities.

The results of these ten items in the specific support index from our three-city survey are presented in Table 3.6. At least two important findings stand out from these results. The first finding is that, in general, our middle-class respondents gave higher "grades" than did the non-middle-class respondents for most of the ten policy areas, although most of the mean grades given by both groups remained in the territory of "so-so" (above or at 3 but under 4). Specifically, the mean scores for eight policy areas (i.e., inflation, job security, housing, social order, medical

Table 3.6 Distribution of Specific Support

	Mean		Standard Deviation	
	Middle Class	Non-middle Class	Middle Class	Non-middle Class
1. Controlling inflation (1–5)[a]	3.4	3.0	0.81	0.83
2. Providing job security (1–5)[a]	3.3	2.7	0.94	1.01
3. Minimizing inequality (1–5)[a]	2.4	2.4	1.03	1.09
4. Improving housing (1–5)[a]	3.0	2.8	0.99	1.01
5. Maintaining order (1–5)[a]	3.6	3.1	0.93	0.96
6. Providing medical care (1–5)[a]	3.8	3.0	0.95	1.02
7. Levying taxes (1–5)[a]	3.4	3.1	0.89	0.89
8. Providing social welfare (1–5)[a]	3.9	3.2	0.93	0.94
9. Combating pollution (1–5)[a]	3.4	3.0	1.03	1.05
10. Fighting corruption (1–5)[a]	2.4	2.4	1.07	1.11
Entire index (10–50)[b]	33.9	28.6	6.56	6.96

[a] For each of the items in this index, respondents were asked to "grade" government policy performance based on the grading scheme commonly used in China's schools on a 1–5 scale, where 1 = very poor, 2 = poor, 3 = so-so, 4 = good, and 5 = very good.
[b] This additive index is constructed by combining all seven items to capture a collective profile of a respondent's specific support, ranging from 10 (indicating very poor policy performance) to 50 (indicating excellent policy performance).
[c] The percentage of positive responses is the combination of the percentage of those who either "agree" or "strongly agree" with the questionnaire statement.

care, taxation, social welfare, and pollution) given by the middle-class respondents were higher than those registered by the non-middle-class respondents. In addition, the mean score for the entire specific support index among the middle-class respondents (33.9) was higher than that among the non-middle-class respondents (28.6).

A second important finding from the results of the ten items in the specific support index is that the views of the middle-class and non-middle-class respondents converged on two policy areas: both groups registered the same, low scores (2.4, which is within the territory of "poor") for "minimizing inequality" and "fighting corruption." This finding confirms many recent observations by China analysts that the majority of the population across class divides perceives the rapidly widening gap between rich and poor and the increasingly rampant official corruption as China's most detestable socio-political problems.

All in all, our major findings about the middle class's political support (or its support for the CCP government) from the three-city survey suggest that compared to the lower class, the middle class tends to be more supportive of the fundamental norms, values, and institutions of the current CCP regime and to respond to the CCP incumbent authorities' policies more favorably. In other words, the middle class seems to be more closely attached to the CCP government in respect to its own ideological orientation and material interests.

C. Correlation Between the Democratic Support and Political Support

I have thus far found that relative to lower class respondents, the middle-class respondents in our sample tended to be less in favor of democratic values and institutions and more supportive of the CCP government. In addition, from the outset of the book, I have proposed that there should be a strong, negative correlation between support for democracy and support for the CCP government: the middle class's attitudes toward democracy and democratization are contingent upon their moral and institutional connections with the current CCP state. Before I test this proposition through a multivariate analysis controlling for several other factors in the next chapter, I will explore this relationship between support for democracy and support for the government through a bivariate analysis. That analysis will help us better understand the more comprehensive multivariate analysis of this core relationship, which follows in the next chapter.

To explore the correlation between the middle class's support for democracy and support for the CCP government through a bivariate analysis, I ran cross-tabulations between the index of democratic support on the one hand and the indexes of the two dimensions of political support on the other hand. Overall, the results of the cross-tabulations (Table 3.7) indicate that both dimensions of political support (or support for the CCP government) were significantly, negatively associated with support for the democratic values and institutions. This finding suggests that among the middle class, those who supported the fundamental norms, values, and institutions of the current CCP regime, and who gave high scores

Table 3.7 Correlation Between Government Support and Democratic Support

	Democratic Support of Middle Class				Democratic Support of Middle Class		
Diffuse Support	**Low (%)**	**Medium (%)**	**High (%)**	**Specific Support**	**Low (%)**	**Medium (%)**	**High (%)**
Low	16	36	57	Low	9	30	51
Medium	32	38	30	Medium	48	60	33
High	52	37	13	High	43	10	16
Total	100	100	100	Total	100	100	100
	gamma = −.692[**]				gamma = −.664[**]		

Note: The additive indexes of diffuse support and democratic values are trichotomized into high, medium, and low levels.
[**]$p < .01$.

for the incumbent authorities' policy performance in major policy areas, tended to be less supportive of democracy and democratization. For instance, while only 13% of those who had a high level of diffuse support for the current CCP regime registered a high level of support for democracy, a majority of those (57%) who had a low level of diffuse support strongly ("high" as indicated in Table 3.7) supported democracy. In addition, whereas only 16% of those who had a high level of specific support strongly supported democracy, a majority (51%) of those who gave a low score for the government policy performance displayed a high level of democratic support. It also should be noted that, as the gamma scores show, the negative correlations between the middle class's support for democracy, on the one hand, and its diffuse support for the current regime (gamma = −.69) along with its specific support for the incumbent authorities (gamma = −.66), on the other hand, were quite strong.

All in all, the results presented in Table 3.7 are consistent with one of the most critical hypotheses I have thus far tried to confirm in this book: that is, the attitudes of the new middle class toward democracy and democratization in today's China depend on this class's moral and material connection with the party-state. We will further explore this central hypothesis, along with other hypotheses, in the chapters that follow.

III. Summary and Conclusion

How much does China's new middle class, relative to the lower class, support a potential political transition toward democracy and the CCP government? What is the relationship between the middle class's attitudes toward democracy and its support for the government? The findings presented throughout this chapter have attempted to address these two questions. It has been found that while most members of this new middle class are in favor of the individual rights that typically are hailed and protected in the democratic system, they shun political liberties such as the freedom to demonstrate and to form organizations. They are neither interested in democratic institutions, such as the fully competitive election of leaders without restriction on political parties, nor enthusiastic about participating in government affairs and politics. Moreover, the middle class is less in favor of the democratic values and institutions identified in this study than the lower class. It has also been found that the low level of the middle class's democratic support correlates with the middle class's support for the current CCP regime and its positive evaluation of incumbent authorities' policy performance. From these findings, it can be inferred that most members of the middle class do not appear to support democratization and democracy in China, in large part due to their close and dependent relationship with the current party-state.

What are the political and theoretical implications of these findings? In terms of political implications, the new middle class in China *now* is unlikely to serve as an agent or supporter of fundamental political change toward democracy. This is not only because most of the class does not seem to support most of the democratic norms and institutions investigated in this study, but also because the middle class as a whole seems to be even less democratically oriented than the lower class. Furthermore, as mentioned earlier, the value and material bonds between the middle class and the state significantly affect the orientation of the middle class toward democratic change. As long as the ruling elite of the state remains determined to maintain the current authoritarian, one-party system, therefore, the middle class is likely to continue to be indifferent to democracy.

As for theoretical implications, compared to the existing studies mentioned earlier (almost none of which was based on probability samples of middle-class individuals in China or other late-developing authoritarian countries), the findings in this chapter provide more robust and conclusive evidence because they are based on data collected from a probability sample of middle-class individuals. Specifically, our findings show that in a late-developing authoritarian country such as China, there is a negative correlation between the middle class's dependence on the state and its support for democracy. While these findings are preliminary, based on a bivariate analysis, they do show a strong possibility—given the strength of bivariate correlations presented previously—that a negative relationship between the middle class's support for democracy and its support for the CCP government may sustain the more robust tests that follow in the next chapter.

4

Why Does or Does Not the Middle Class Support Democracy?

IN THE PREVIOUS chapter, I depicted the levels of the middle class's support for democracy, as well as its support for the Chinese Communist Party (CCP) government, in comparison with the levels of such support within the lower class. Findings presented in that chapter showed that compared to the respondents in the lower class, those in the middle class are less supportive of democracy and democratization, but are more supportive of the current authoritarian government. In the previous chapter, I also explored the relationship between the middle class's support for democracy and its support for the CCP government, through a bivariate analysis. I found that there is quite a strong, negative correlation between these two kinds of support among the middle-class respondents. Based on these important findings, this chapter will examine the *set* of sociopolitical factors expected to influence the middle class's attitudes toward democracy and democratization in China. By examining these factors, I attempt to answer a fundamental question based on the data collected from both the probability-sample survey and in-depth interviews conducted in the three cities: why does or does not the middle class support democracy?

Following the logic of the contingent approach discussed in chapter 1, I suggest that China's middle class's attitudinal orientations toward democracy and democratization are contingent upon salient socioeconomic and sociopolitical conditions that affect this social class, at both individual and societal levels. Particularly, I focus on two categories of major socioeconomic and sociopolitical factors that I believe have significantly affected the middle class's democratic support. These factors include the middle class's ideational and institutional connections with the incumbent authoritarian state and its evaluations of its own social and economic well-being. While these two categories of factors by no means exhaust all the causes of the middle class's support for democracy, examining them can allow for a test of some key propositions from previous studies of the middle classes in late-developing countries. The results of the test will provide a better understanding of the middle class's democratic support in China, as well as other, similar late-developing countries. The hypothesized impact of these two categories of factors, as independent variables, and the potential influence of some control variables on the middle class's democratic support are explained below.

A. The Dependence on the State

To reiterate key arguments from the extant studies that have been summarized in Chapter 1, Alexander Gerschenkron (1962) argues that in a late-developing country,[1] the state normally plays a more important role than does the state in an early-industrialized country in the process of socioeconomic development. This is mainly because, as Gercshenkron points out, late-developing countries need a strong state to compensate for the inadequate supplies of capital, entrepreneurship, and technological capacity possessed by these countries, in order to compete with early-industrialized countries and survive global competition.

Consistent with this notion of the role of the state in late-developing countries, some analysts argue that the state in a late-developing country also plays a decisive role in creating social classes, such as the new middle classes, and hence in shaping their socioeconomic and political traits (Bell 1998; Johnson 1985; Jones 1998; Shin 1999). Consequently, "the state [also] became important in shaping the political articulation of newly emerging social forces" (Rueschemeyer, Stephens, and Stephens 1992, 223). Following this theoretical line, some scholars argue that the new middle class in late-developing countries not only is dependent upon the state for its rise and growth but also shares common interests with the state (e.g., Sundhaussen 1991; Brown and Jones 1995; Bell 1998). In a late-developing country, therefore, the middle class is likely to support the state and the political system that is sanctioned by the state and in which the state operates. As a result, if a political system is undemocratic in a given country, its middle class tends to turn its back on democratization to avoid antagonizing the state.

As in other late-developing countries, China's new middle class has a dependent relationship with the state. Yet the state in China is even more effective than that in other late-developing countries in controlling the society and creating/shaping new social classes, including the middle class, as well as private entrepreneurs (or "capitalists").[2] This is because the Chinese state rests upon two unique, powerful pillars that other late-developing countries do not usually have: the dominance of the single, Leninist party—the CCP—and a prerogative to intervene in any socioeconomic sphere (Walder 1995a). With these two pillars, the party-state effectively facilitated the emergence and growth of a new middle class in both the private and public sectors. As a result, this class is more dependent on the party-state.

First of all, due to the dominant role of the party-state in influencing the career and life opportunities of the middle class, at least one-half of that class is still employed in the public sector, such as government and party agencies, state-owned enterprises, and public organizations (e.g., Zheng and Li 2004). Furthermore, both the state and the middle class share fundamental interests: promotion of economic growth, protection of private property, maintenance of social stability, and restriction of mass political participation (particularly by those in the lower class who still constitute the majority of the population) (e.g., Chen 2002; Goodman 1999; Xiao 2003). As David G. Goodman (1999, 260–261) argues, the Chinese middle class, in general, is "far from being alienated from the party-state or seeking their own political voice, and appears to be operating in close proximity and through close cooperation" with the party-state.

In general, therefore, it is expected that the middle class's connections with and dependence on China's incumbent authoritarian state is negatively associated with its attitudes toward democracy and democratization. In other words, the relatively low level of democratic support (presented earlier in this book) among the middle-class respondents may be mainly caused by a high level of their connections with and dependence on the state. Moreover, these connections and dependence may play a more important role for the middle class than the lower class in lowering support for a democratization that could threaten the current party-state, since the former has benefited more from the connections and dependence than has the latter. Drawing on data from the three-city survey, I explore this proposition about the correlations between the middle class's democratic support, on the one hand, and its value congruence with, and employment/career dependence on, the state, on the other. These correlations are further specified as follows.

Impact of Value Congruence. The middle class's value congruence with the CCP state can be measured by the two dimensions of political support among the middle class: (1) diffuse support for the fundamental norms, values, and institutions of the current regime and (2) specific support for the policy performance of the incumbent authorities in major policy areas. It is believed that citizens are linked to the regime by diffuse support, which stems from their assessment of the fundamental values, norms, and institutions of the government; citizens are connected to the incumbent political authorities through their specific support, which is derived from their perceptions and evaluations of the actual policy outputs of the authorities (see Easton 1965, 1976). I believe that this value congruence—here operationalized as the two dimensions of political support—serves as the foundation of the tie between the current party-state and the middle class in China. As presented in the previous chapter, the results of political support from our sample indicate that relative to the lower class, the middle-class respondents enjoyed *higher* levels of both diffuse support and specific support for the CCP state.

There seems to be a consensus in field observations by China scholars (e.g., Nathan 1990, 1997, 2008; Baum 1994; Ogden 2002; Chen 2004; Pei 2006) suggesting that since the onset of the post-Mao reforms, the party-state has to a large extent relaxed its control over citizens' private lives. But the consensus also maintains that this post-Mao regime has been far from democratic, because it has by no means given up one-party rule nor ceased its harsh repression of political dissidents. Overall, the current Chinese regime's norms and practices have thus far worked against most democratic norms and principles investigated in this study, such as the rights to demonstrate and assemble and to participate in government affairs, as well as competitive elections with multiple-party competition (Pei 2006). As I discussed in the previous chapter, therefore, I expect that those middle-class respondents who support the current regime are unlikely to support democratic norms and institutions.

To further explore the relationship between the two dimensions of political support for the current regime and support for democracy among the middle class, I ran a partial correlation analysis. In this analysis, I examined the correlation between political support and democratic support among our respondents, controlling for several key sociodemographic variables, such as sex, age, and education. I wanted to see if our hypothesized correlation between political support and democratic support could sustain the impact of those demographic factors. These results, presented in Table 4.1, include two kinds of correlations between democratic support and the two dimensions of political support (or diffuse

Table 4.1 Partial Correlations Between Support for Democracy and Support for the Chinese Communist Party Government

	Democratic Support and Diffuse Support	Democratic Support and Specific Support
(1) Correlation coefficient (r)	.79*	.59*
(2) Partial correlation coefficient (r)		
Sex	.77*	.56*
Age	.71*	.60*
Education	.80*	.61*
All of the above	.74*	.57*

Note: All questionnaire items for democratic support and those for each of the two dimensions of political support are combined to form additive indexes, respectively: support for democracy, diffuse support, and specific support. Sex: male = 0; female = 1. Education: middle school and below = 1; high school = 2; post-secondary professional training = 3; four-year university education = 4; graduate level = 5.

*$p < .05$.

support and specific support): the correlations *before* and *after* controlling for the sociodemographic variables. As can be seen in the table, there are virtually no substantial differences between these two kinds of correlations. Apparently, therefore, the key sociodemographic factors examined here exerted *little* meaningful influence, either individually or collectively, on the relationships between democratic support and the two dimensions of political support among the middle-class respondents. Thus, one can conclude that the strong, negative correlation between support for democracy and support for the CCP government persisted across such major sociodemographic categories as age, income, educational level, and sex in our sample. This finding suggests that the durability of this relationship extends beyond the influence of demographic factors. In China, while sociodemographic factors may in fact influence middle-class individuals' support for democracy as well as their support for the CCP government, they do not seem to influence, in any meaningful way, the overall

relationship between democratic support and government support. Throughout this study, therefore, this strong negative relationship of democratic support with government support can be
treated as a sort of universal phenomenon across the major sociodemographic attributes among the middle class.

The middle class's value congruence with the CCP state can also
be measured by its attitudes toward "political reform." To measure the Chinese middle class's evaluation of political reform, we
asked respondents to assess a statement: "China currently needs
a major political reform." They were asked to assess this statement on a five-point scale, where 1 stands for strong disagreement
with the statement and 5 refers to strong agreement with it. A
clear majority (about 67%) of our middle-class respondents either
disagreed or strongly disagreed with this statement (not shown in
a table). In other words, most members of the middle class in our
survey seemed to want to maintain the political status quo of CCP
rule.

I argue that such attitudes toward political reform are associated with one's desire for democracy in post-Mao China.
Over the past two decades, political reform in post-Mao China
has emphasized political rationalization and legalization
(McCormick 1990). Specifically, the post-Mao reformist government under Deng Xiaoping abandoned Mao's practices of class
struggle and continuous revolution under the "proletarian dictatorship," rebuilt the party and governmental apparatus as a
modern bureaucracy, strengthened "socialist legality," and loos-
ened controls over the private lives of ordinary citizens. Any
deepening of such seemingly partial and rudimentary political
reforms will naturally require a fundamental change of government norms and institutions—from "communist" authoritarian
norms and institutions to more democratic ones. Any further
political reform therefore should be understood to mean further liberalization and democratization of Chinese political culture and structure, making the decision-making process more
transparent and public officials more accountable to the general

public. Some earlier studies of the Chinese setting have found that Chinese citizens who desire further political reform are likely to support potential democratization (Chen and Zhong 1998). Therefore, I hypothesize that the middle-class individuals who demand further political reform are more likely to support democratic values than those who do not feel the need for further political reform.

To explore the hypothesized relationship between a perceived need for further political reform and support for democracy, I ran a cross-tabulation between the index of democratic support and the statement above regarding the middle class's attitudes toward political reform. The results of this analysis (Table 4.2) are consistent with our expectation: that is, those who disagreed or strongly disagreed with the statement that "China currently needs a major political reform" were less likely to support a shift toward democracy. Specifically, over 60% of the respondents who did not feel the need for any future political reform showed little or no support for democracy and democratization, while only about 6% of them were strongly supportive of democracy; in contrast, 56% of those who wanted further political reform displayed strong support for democratic values and norms, while only about 12% of them registered

Table 4.2 Support for Democracy and Satisfaction with the Pace of Political Reform

Perceived Need for Further Political Reform	Level of Support for Democracy			
	Low	Medium	High	Total
Agree/strongly agree (%)	11.6	32.2	56.2	100
Disagree/strongly disagree (%)	61.7	32.7	5.6	100
	gamma = .79*			

Note: The index of support for democracy is trichotomized into three categories: low, medium, and high. The question about perceived need for political reform is dichotomized: the combination of "disagree" and "strongly disagree," and the combination of "agree" and "strongly agree."
*$p < .05$.

a low level of support for such values and norms. This relationship between the perceived need for political reform and democratic support was also substantiated by a strong correlation coefficient (gamma = .79). In short, these results suggest that the middle class's lack of support for democracy may result from its lack of desire for any further political change, which might bring about the collapse of the current CCP regime.

Impact of Employment/Career Dependence. It has long been argued that one's employment status and work settings may influence a person's political attitudes. Based on a comparative study of the variation in political attitudes within the middle class, for example, Erik Wright (1997, 464) suggests that people in different sectors of the same class "could have very different interests (material as well as non-material interests) by virtue of the constraints and possibilities they confront, and these interests could in turn underwrite different ideological orientations." This is because, according to Wright (1997, 465–467), "different employment settings could be characterized by conditions encouraging different degrees of cognitive complexity or generating various forms of cognitive dissonance which in turn would affect ideological dispositions. More broadly, the 'lived experience' within different kinds of work settings shape ideology." Thus, Wright argues that "within the middle class, people employed in state services will hold more prostatist attitudes...than will people in...the private sector;" "because of their dependency on state employment, we would expect the middle class in the state services to be more prostatist" (Wright 1997, 466). Can this general argument be supported by our study of the middle class in China?

As mentioned earlier, the state in China has played an even more preponderant role in influencing the career and life opportunities of the newly rising middle class than have states in non-communist, late-developing countries. Using its unchallengeable (or almost absolute) political power and pervasive institutions, the party-state has not only created a general socioeconomic environment that is conducive to the emergence and growth of this social class as a whole but also provided its members with jobs and career opportunities within the state apparatus. In my survey, for example, a majority (about 60%) of middle-class respondents were employed in the state apparatus at the time of our survey.[3]

More important, access to these positions and opportunities is subject to party membership and/or political loyalty to the party-state (e.g., Lu 2002, 2004; Zhang 2005; Zheng and Li 2004). As a result, the state can directly and effectively influence the political attitudes of the middle class through the provision of employment and career opportunities. As Andrew Walder (1995b, 309) argues, the party-state's power "to offer career opportunities has long been recognized as a central pillar of Communist rule, either as a system of social control (rewards for loyalty) or as a means of fostering anticipatory socialization and (at least outward) ideological conformity." Thus, we expect that those of this class who are employed in the *state apparatus* (including government and party agencies, state-owned enterprises and public organizations) are more likely to identify themselves with the party-state and hence less likely to support democracy and democratization.

To explore this expectation, I ran a bivariate analysis of the correlation between the employment in the state apparatus and support for democracy among the middle-class respondents in this survey. As shown in Table 4.3, those who were employed in

Table 4.3 Support for Democracy and Employment Status

Employment Status	Level of Support for Democracy			
	Low	Medium	High	Total
State employment (%)	51.3	37.3	11.3	100
Non-state employment (%)	13.7	36.4	49.9	100
	gamma = −.79*			

Note: The index of support for democracy is trichotomized into three categories: low, medium, and high.
*$p < .05$.

the state apparatus tended to be less supportive of democratic values and institutions, while those who were employed outside of the state apparatus were more likely to be in favor of such values and institutions. For example, over 50% of state employees expressed a low level of support for democracy, while only 11% of them registered a high level of such support. But on the other hand, about 50% of non-state employees had a high level of democratic support and only about 14% of them enjoyed a low level of such support. The results of this analysis support our expectation that there is a strong and negative relationship (gamma = −.79) between democratic support and employment in the state apparatus.

Such results can be supported by the in-depth interviews of middle-class individuals. Consider this story of a member of the middle class who was employed in the private sector and showed a strong support for democracy.

Mr. 133 had run his law firm for more than ten years in the city of Chengdu in Western China.[4] He graduated from a very well-regarded law school in Beijing. Upon graduation, he went to Chengdu to work as a lawyer. Several years later, he had accumulated enough capital to open his own law firm. We met him in his fancy and spacious office. After a cup of coffee (note: drinking coffee is considered part of the middle-class life style in China), he started his story of running a law firm in that city. He was quite angry with government corruption; so when we moved to the topic of democracy, Mr. 133 clearly expressed his view of democracy:

Democracy means freedom and happiness. If we can have democracy, then we can have the right to choose. Every citizen is enthusiastic about democracy. Though there are some elections in China, participation is insufficient. Democracy is of course a good thing. Only democracy can make the government open and fair. There is no doubt that democracy is also good for China, because the democratic countries have proven

to be the most economically developed in the world. One example of a democratic system is America. In the United States,
everyone has his or her own interests, and everyone can vote
based on his or her own interests. Now in China, we find it difficult to punish the corrupt officials, because we do not have
elections or democracy to check them.

When we discussed the relationship between electoral democracy and potential instability in China, Mr. 133 said:

I do not think that electoral democracy will create instability
in China. Citizens should have their right to vote. Voting is
to express their interests and their voices. The fairness and
openness of procedures of the rule are very important. The
openness of the procedures and results of the elections can
prevent social disorder. Our current political system lacks
such openness, and should be changed.

B. Impact of the Perceived Social and Economic Well-Being

Many studies of the middle class in developing countries point
out that the attitudes of the social groups toward democratization and democracy are contingent upon their perception
of their own social and economic conditions under the incumbent regimes (Koo 1991; Sundhaussen 1991; Hadiz 2004; Chen
2002; Englehart 2003; Thompson 2004). Perhaps such perceived
socioeconomic well-being has a significant and "near-universal"
(Rueschemeyer, Stephens, and Stephens 1992, 60) impact on
middle classes' support for democracy in *both* earlier industrialized and late-developing countries. As Ulf Sundhaussen
(1991, 112) argues, the middle class "would, obviously, not have
backed moves towards democracy if this would have meant losing their wealth and privileges." In other words, in both the
earlier industrialized and late-developing societies, the middle
class judged democratization largely based on the perceived

consequences of such political change for their own social and economic well-being.

More pertinent to our study, many analysts of the middle classes' democratic support in late-developing countries have found that these classes in general are less likely to initiate or support democratization under authoritarian regimes when they are satisfied with their own social and economic status. For example, some of these analysts found that in the developing countries of East/Southeast Asia, such as South Korea, Taiwan, Singapore, Indonesia, and Malaysia, as long as the new middle classes remained clear "beneficiaries" of state-led economic development, they were not motivated to initiate or support political change toward democracy; however, once their socioeconomic gains were perceived to be fading, the middle classes might agitate for or participate in political movements challenging the regimes under which they lived (Jones 1998; Shwarz 1994; Tamura 2003; Torii 2003). These findings about the contingency of the middle class's attitudes to democracy and democratization also seem to fit the second-largest developing country, India. As Leela Fernandes (2006, 186–187) has observed, when middle-class citizens in that country perceived that "their interests are not being served by politicians and by the state," many of them turned their backs on the existing democracy, contending that India "needs a dictator."

More important, some scholars of China have also found that members of the middle class in that country seem to link their views of democracy to their perceived socioeconomic interests (Goodman 1999; Chen 2002; Xiao 2003; Zheng and Li 2004; Zhang 2005; Wright 2010). For instance, one of these scholars (Wright 2010, 83–84) has observed that the state-led economic reform and development in the post-Mao era "over time have led most of China's [middle class] to enjoy a comfortable life style and a high socioeconomic status relative to other groups. At the same time, they have become formally independent of the state. Rather than causing [the middle class] to question the legitimacy of single-party rule, these developments have made most skeptical of majority rule and desirous of close connections to the existing authoritarian political establishment." In addition,

> because [members of the middle class] are part of the minority that sits at the upper level of China's highly polarized socioeconomic structure, they have had little cause to support the political empowerment of the masses. In addition, inasmuch as the ruling CCP has served as a vehicle for economic success, professionals have had incentives to join it and to work within its structures—both to maintain and to promote their own prosperity. (Wright 2010, 83–84)

This observation has been confirmed by one of the most renowned China-based social scientists, who observes: "the stake that these [middle-class] people held in the booming economy hardly made them adventurous political reformists; on the contrary, they worried that too much political change too fast could…endanger their material interests" (Xiao 2003, 62). Based on all these observations in authoritarian, late-developing societies including China, therefore, I expect that those in the middle class in contemporary China who are satisfied with their current social and economic statuses are even less likely to support political shakeups for democracy than are those in the lower class.

To measure the Chinese middle class's satisfaction with social and economic status, I used two questions in the three-city survey, as follows:

1. Overall, how satisfied are you with your social status?
2. Overall, how satisfied are you with your economic status?

The respondents were asked to answer each of the two questions on a five-point scale (with 1 = very dissatisfied, 2 = dissatisfied, 3 = so-so, 4 = satisfied, and 5 = very satisfied).[5] As the results from both questions indicated (Table 4.4), the middle-class respondents were more satisfied with their social and economic statuses than

Table 4.4 Satisfaction with Social and Economic Statuses

	Mean Score Among the Middle Class	Mean Score Among the Non-middle Class
Overall, please evaluate how satisfied you were with your social status. (1–5)	4.1	3.1*
Overall, please evaluate how satisfied you were with your economic status. (1–5)	3.8	2.6*

Note: The respondents were asked to answer each of the two questions on a five-point scale (with 1 = very dissatisfied, 2 = dissatisfied, 3 = so-so, 4 = satisfied, and 5 = very satisfied). A factor analysis was conducted of these two items in the responses of both classes. From the factor analysis, only one dominant factor emerged, which explained 65% of the original variance. Approximate Ns of the middle-class respondents are 739, whereas the Ns of non-middle-class respondents (excluding private entrepreneurs or capitalists and ranking government officials) are 2,330.

* Difference between the responses by the middle class and by the non-middle class is significant at the .05 level.

were the non-middle-class respondents. Specifically, the mean scores given by those in the middle class for both social and economic statuses (4.1 and 3.8, respectively) were significantly (at the 0.5 level) higher than the corresponding scores given by those in the non-middle class (3.1 and 2.6, respectively). In other words, it can be said that during the time of our surveys between 2007 and 2008, the middle class was much happier with its social and economic statuses than were members of the lower class in the three major cities, Beijing, Chengdu, and Xian.

The results from the probability-sample survey can be supported by what was found from the in-depth interviews of middle-class individuals. Among these individuals, those employed in the state sector seemed to be the most satisfied with their social and economic statuses. Here is a story of a member of the middle class who was employed in a state-owned enterprise.[6]

In his mid-fifties, Mr. 63 was a mid-level manager in a state-owned enterprise in Beijing. He had worked in this enterprise for more than thirty years, and the interview was carried out in his nice four-bedroom apartment. He began by talking about his miserable childhood:

> My childhood was miserable. I was born before the Great Leap Forward. Therefore, I had very little to eat in my childhood. My parents could not raise me and sent me to a rich family. Later on, when I grew up, my parents got me back from that family. Because of the Cultural Revolution, I could not finish my middle school education. I came to this enterprise in 1970, and worked as an apprentice. After that, I became a full worker.

But when we discussed his current living conditions, Mr. 63 was quite satisfied with his economic status. He was making an annual income of more than 180,000 yuan (equivalent to $27,000). Commenting on his salary, Mr. 63 told us that "my salary is good. Of course, I am not very rich. But I am very content with my current financial status, compared to my miserable childhood. In addition, my job is very stable." In 1998, he bought a 100-square-meter apartment from his enterprise at a below-market-value price. In 2002, he bought his second apartment, a four-bedroom one, at the market price. At the time of the interview, these two apartments together were valued at more than five million *yuan* (equivalent to more than $750,000). He also owned a fancy Toyota Reiz and had sent his son to Peking University, one of the most prestigious universities in China, for his higher education.

When our interview turned to the issue of social status, Mr. 63 sounded even more confident:

> Now, in China, there are many discussions of the middle class. I think I belong to that class. I have two fancy apartments, drive a nice car, and have a comfortable life, as well as a decent job. I guess that is what the Chinese middle class all will have. In

addition, my job provides me with a very decent social status. Look at my social networks. Most of my friends have the same life style as mine. On weekends, we often together drive our cars to the countryside for barbecues. Most people in society look up to us.

Consider another member of the middle class in the in-depth interview study, who was employed in a foreign company.[7] In her early thirties, Ms. 126 was a financial analyst in a foreign company, also living in Beijing. We began our interview by talking about her job. She said:

My job is very decent, and my salary is quite good. Every day, I wear fashionable clothes and sit in this fancy office. My annual income is about 400,000 yuan (equivalent to $55,000). In addition, my company provides me with very good health insurance and a pension plan. Compared to my college classmates, my income is very high.

But unlike Mr. 63, who was employed in a state-owned enterprise, Ms. 126 clearly lacked a sense of financial security. She explained:

I don't have any feeling of job security. If one day I lost this job, I don't know what sort of job I could find or when, so I must save money. Many of my classmates work in government agencies or state-owned enterprises, and even though their salaries are lower than mine, they have job security. In addition, they can buy apartments from their work units at a below-market-value price.

Toward the end of our interview, when asked to evaluate her own social status, Ms. 126 said:

My social status looks good. But in reality I don't have many things to be proud of. I have a good salary, which probably is the only thing that I can be proud of. However, my future doesn't look very bright: someday I will get old, and lose my job. If that happens, I will become very miserable. My friends in the government or state-owned enterprises might have a better future: when they get old, they will get a promotion; after they have power, they will become important figures in this society. While I am definitely better off than those in the lower class, I still don't feel I enjoy the same social status as my white-collar friends in state-owned enterprises.

Furthermore, to explore the hypothesis that those in the middle class who are satisfied with their current social and economic statuses are even less likely to support a political shakeup for the sake of democracy than are those in the lower class, I ran a bivariate analysis (cross-tabulation) between these two variables. The results presented in Table 3.6 confirm that there is a significant, negative correlation (gamma = −.69) between democratic support and perceived well-being among the middle class. That is, those who were satisfied with their social and economic statuses were less likely to support democracy and democratization. As shown in Table 4.5,

Table 4.5 Correlations Between Support for Democracy and Perceived Social and Economic Well-Being Among the Middle Class

	Support for Democracy		
Perceived Well-Being	**Low %**	**Medium %**	**High %**
Low	6.5	18.0	48.2
Medium	35.4	44.5	35.2
High	58.1	37.5	16.6
TOTAL	100	100	100
	gamma = −.69*		

Note: All questionnaire items of the variable for democratic support and those of the variable for perceived social and economic well-being are combined to formed two additive indexes, respectively: support for democracy and perceived well-being. Then, each of these two indexes is trichotomized into three categories: high, intermediate, and low levels.
*$p < .05$.

a majority (about 60%) of those who were highly content with their statuses scored "low" for democratic support.

C. Control Variables

Do the middle class's connections with and dependence on the state, as measured by value congruence and employment/career dependence, and its perception of its socioeconomic well-being influence the middle class's support for democratization and democracy *independently* of some other factors that may also have an effect on democratic support? To answer this question, I include in this analysis two categories of factors as control variables: (1) key sociodemographic attributes and (2) local socioeconomic conditions.

Sociodemographic Attributes. A large body of the literature on democratic values in both Chinese and non-Chinese settings suggests that certain key sociodemographic attributes may influence middle-class individuals' attitudes toward democracy (e.g., Glassman 1991, 1995, 1997; Lipset 1981; Chen 2004). This is mainly because these sociodemographic attributes are considered to play a significant role in shaping the process of political socialization, which in turn may affect the middle class's attitudes toward democracy. Drawing upon these earlier studies, therefore, I include key sociodemographic attributes as control variables, such as sex, age, education, Communist Party membership, and income. I suspect that along with the three independent variables specified earlier, these sociodemographic attributes may also impact middle-class people's support for democratization and democracy.

Local Socioeconomic Conditions. In our survey study, we selected three major cities, Beijing, Chengdu, and Xi'an, to represent approximately three levels of economic development in urban China. While Beijing represents the cities with a high per capita GDP, Chengdu and Xi'an are indicative of those with a medium and a low per capita GDP, respectively. According to modernization theory, the middle class in a more advanced economy is more likely than that in a less advanced economy to support democratization and democracy, because the middle class in a more advanced economy is more likely to become a sizable social group. It is therefore less likely to feel threatened by the lower class and more likely to feel confident about its potential political role in a democratic political system (e.g., Fukuyama 1993; Glassman 1995, 1997; Lipset 1959, 1981).

In addition, it is commonly assumed that the various social conditions unique to each of these three cities—which are located in China's Northeast (Beijing), Northwest (Xi'an), and Southwest (Chengdu)—may influence our respondents' views about social and political issues. This is simply because variations in the social conditions in these three cities—along with the sociodemographic factors mentioned earlier—are likely to cause the disparities in people's political socialization processes in the three locales. Thus, I suspect that residence in a particular city may have an impact on our respondents' attitudes toward democracy. It could be expected that residents in Beijing would be more supportive of democracy than those in Xi'an or Chengdu, since Beijing is more cosmopolitan and has more access to the West than either of the other two cities.

In short, I suspect that the difference among the three cities in their levels of economic development and in their levels of social conditions could influence support for democracy among the middle class. Specifically, the middle-class respondents in Beijing could have the highest level of democratic support, while those in Xi'an could have the lowest level of such support.

II. Results of the Multivariate Analyses

Thus far, I have employed *bivariate* analytical techniques (e.g., cross-tabulation and bivariate coefficient) to explore the hypothesized relationships between democratic support as the dependent variable, on the one hand, and membership in the middle class and this class's connections with the state and its perceived well-being as the independent variables, on the other hand. While the results from the bivariate analyses presented earlier support my theoretical hypotheses, these results need to be further verified by a multivariate analysis that can determine the independent effect of each of the independent variables.

To determine this independent effect, therefore, I ran a multiple regression model (OLS) based on the entire sample of our three-city survey,[8] which encompassed both the middle-class and lower class respondents. This model included all the major categories of explanatory variables (i.e., value congruence, career dependence, and perceived well-being), along with the control variables. It also included a dummy variable for membership in the middle class to confirm the impact of that membership on democratic support in general, as well as the interactive terms between membership in the middle class and the key explanatory variables to test the hypothesized relationships (or interactions) between the explanatory variables and middle-class membership. Table 4.6 presents the results of this multiple regression model. Overall, these results are consistent with expectations: even independently of some key sociodemographic attributes and local socioeconomic conditions, (1) membership in the middle class influences democratic support throughout the entire sample, and (2) the middle class's ideational and material connections with the state, and its satisfaction with its personal social and economic statuses affect this class's orientation toward democracy.

First of all, as expected earlier and as indicated in the bivariate analysis previously, the results presented in Table 4.6 confirmed that membership in the middle class did significantly and negatively affect respondents' attitudes toward democracy in our sample. In other words, those who belonged to the middle class were much less likely than those in the lower class to support democracy and democratization in China.

In terms of the effects of value congruence, as I expected, not only did both diffuse support and specific support for the CCP

Table 4.6 Multivariate Regression of Support for Democratic Values and Institutions Among Middle-Class Respondents: Beijing, Chengdu, and Xi'an

	Support for Democratic Values and Institutions[a]		
	b	s.e.	beta
Class Indicator			
• Middle-class membership[b]	−.538**	.231	−.149
Relationship with the state			
• Diffuse support[c]	−.923**	.117	−.145
• Specific support[d]	−.645**	.081	−.136
• Diffuse support × membership in the middle class (interactive term)	−.177*	.081	−.066
• Specific support × membership in the middle class (interactive term)	−.141*	.075	−.061
• Support for major political reform	.346**	.108	.081
• Support for major political reform × membership in the middle class (interactive term)	.576*	.312	.032
• Employment in the state apparatus[e]	−1.232**	.275	−.113
• Employment in the state apparatus × membership in the middle class (interactive term)	−.520*	.298	−.046
Socioeconomic well-being			
• Satisfaction with social and economic status[f]	−.452**	.098	−.086
• Satisfaction with social and economic status × membership in the middle class (interactive term)	−.778*	.312	−.033
Control variables			
• Sex[g]	−.339**	.169	−.034
• Age	−.001	.008	−.002
• Education[h]	.927**	.125	.163
• Household gross income[i]	.541**	.162	.073
• Party membership[j]	−.370	.278	−.019

(Continued)

Table 4.6 (Continued)

	Support for Democratic Values and Institutions[a]		
	b	s.e.	beta
· Location[k]			
Beijing	.387	.536	.028
Chengdu	−.924	.721	−.021
Constant	41.421**	1.733	
R^2	.294		
Adjusted R^2	.278		
N	2,810		

Note: **p* < .05; ***p* < .01; *b* = unstandardized coefficient; beta = standardized coefficient.

[a] The value of support for democratic values and institutions is the factor score of the four subdimensions.

[b] Lower class = 0; middle class = 1.

[c] The value of diffuse support is the factor score of the seven items.

[d] The value of specific support is the factor score of the eleven items.

[e] The state apparatus here included government and party agencies, state-owned enterprises, and public organizations. Employment in the state apparatus = 1; employment outside of the state apparatus = 0.

[f] The value of satisfaction with social and economic status is the factor score of the two items.

[g] Male = 0; female = 1.

[h] Middle school and below = 1; high school = 2; post-secondary professional training = 3; four-year university education = 4; graduate level = 5.

[i] The original value of household gross income was transformed to the base-e logarithm value.

[j] We asked respondents to answer the following question: "Are you a member of the Communist Party?" Non-party member = 0; party member = 1.

[k] Xi'an is set as a reference group.

government have a significant, negative effect on the orientation toward democratic principles and institutions within the general population, but also, more important, this negative effect was more pronounced among members of the middle class.[9] These results suggest that middle-class respondents scoring higher in support for the current party-state were less supportive of democratic principles and institutions than were those lower class respondents who also expressed high diffuse support. Similarly, consistent with our earlier expectation, those who did not support a major political reform tended to be against democracy and democratization; those in the middle class who did not support political reform were even less likely to favor democracy than were *all* the respondents in the lower class and those in the middle class who supported political reform.

As for the impact of employment/career dependence, the results in Table 4.6 indicated that there was a significant, negative correlation between employment in the state apparatus and support for democracy and democratization within the general population. In other words, those employed by the state sector (government and party agencies, state-owned enterprises, and public organizations) were less likely to support democracy than those who worked outside the state sector. More important, the results also showed that the negative effect of employment in the state apparatus on democratic support was much stronger among members of the middle class than among members of the lower class.[10] Thus, it can be said that those middle-class individuals employed by the state sector were less likely to support democracy than were those in the lower class working in the state apparatus, those in the middle class but not employed in the state apparatus, and those neither employed in the state sector nor in the middle class. These findings are in accordance with our earlier expectation: middle-class identity and state-employment status together have a greater effect than just middle-class identity or state-employment status alone.

With respect to the impact of the perceived social and economic well-being, the results in Table 4.6 indicated that in general, there was a significant, negative correlation between satisfaction with social and economic status and support for democracy within the general population. This suggested that the more satisfied people were with their social and economic conditions, the less supportive they were of democratic change. Furthermore, like the impact of the other independent variables mentioned earlier, the negative effect of status satisfaction on democratic support was stronger among members of the middle class than it was among those of the lower class.[11] It can be said, therefore, that those middle-class individuals who were satisfied with their own social and economic status were much less likely to support democracy and democratization in China than were those lower class citizens who were similarly satisfied.

Based on these findings, one may conclude that ideational congruence with the party-state, employment in the state apparatus, and satisfaction with one's social and economic statuses play a more important role for the middle class than they do for the lower class in lowering support for democracy and democratization. Because the middle class has benefited more from the current regime and has been more dependent upon the state than the lower class, the middle class is less likely to support democratization than the lower class.

Finally, among the control variables, education, household gross income, and party membership have a significant effect on democratic support. Specifically, both middle-class and lower-class respondents who were female, who had higher education, and who possessed higher household income tended to be more supportive of democratic values. It is worth noting that the difference among local socioeconomic conditions (Beijing, Chengdu, and Xi'an) did not have a significant impact on the attitudes toward democracy. This finding is not consistent with modernization theory, which stresses a significant, positive relationship between the level of economic development and support for democracy. The possible reason for this inconsistency certainly deserves a separate and more thorough study, which requires more information than just these proxy indicators (i.e., locations).

III. Summary and Conclusion

Why does or does not this social class support political change? The findings presented throughout this chapter have attempted to address this question. The low level of the middle class's democratic support correlates with the two key categories of variables investigated in this study: (1) the middle class's ideational and institutional connections with the state (i.e., diffuse support and specific support for the CCP government, lack of desire for further political reform, and employment/career dependence on the state) and (2) the middle class's assessment of its own economic and social statuses under the current party-state system. From these findings, it can be inferred that most members of the middle class do not appear to support democratization and democracy in China largely because of their close and dependent relationship with the current party-state, as well as their general satisfaction with their own social and economic conditions under the current regime.

What are the political and theoretical implications of our findings? In terms of political implications, given the causal relationship established in this chapter between the middle class's ideational and material dependence on the party-state and its perceived socioeconomic conditions on the one hand and this class's democratic support on the other hand, the middle class may become enthusiastic about democratization and democracy *only if* such dependence is significantly weakened and socioeconomic conditions deteriorate. Thus, it can be said that among other factors, the state's enduring failure to deliver economic growth, maintain social stability, and increase or maintain employment/career opportunities and living standards for the middle class may help drive the middle class to support political change toward democracy.

As for theoretical implications, our findings show that in a late-developing authoritarian country such as China, (1) there is a negative correlation between the middle class's dependence on the state and its support for democracy, and (2) the middle class's perceived social and economic well-being is also negatively associated with its democratic support. These findings have at least indirectly challenged the unilinear approach, which argues that economic development inevitably leads to—among other modern sociopolitical phenomena—the emergence of a new middle class, and that the creation of this social class in turn promotes democratization. The evidence from this study, to the contrary, indicates that the middle class is *not* necessarily enthusiastic about democratization and democracy in an authoritarian, late-developing country due to its dependence on the state and its concern over socioeconomic well-being.

5

The Impact of Democratic Support on the Middle Class's Political Behavior

THUS FAR I have focused on the levels and sources of the *attitudes* of China's middle class toward democracy, as well as the current Chinese Communist Party (CCP) government. Do these attitudes significantly influence the middle class's political behavior or political participation in China? If so, how? This chapter answers these crucial questions. The answers to the questions have direct implications for the prospects for democratic change, as well as for the fate of the current CCP government in China.

To answer these two key questions in this chapter, I will first explore the major forms and intensity of the middle class's political participation based on the data collected from the three cities and then explore the impact of the middle class's attitudes toward democracy and toward the CCP government on the political participation of the middle class. As discussed in chapter 1, although the descriptive results from the three-city survey about the forms and intensity may not be generalized directly to the entire country, the findings about the causal relationships between democratic support on the one hand and the forms and intensity of political participation among the middle class on the other may have some general implications for the causes of the middle class's political behavior in today's China. These implications will be addressed in this chapter.

I. Major Forms and Intensity of Political Participation

Since the outset of post-Mao economic and political reforms in China in the late 1970s, more and more ordinary citizens, including those in the middle class, have reportedly participated in public affairs and politics, even though China's political system has never been democratic, especially by Western standards (Tang and Parish 2000; Chen and Zhong 2002; Zhong and Chen 2002; Chen 2004). To understand the impact of the middle class's attitudes toward democracy and toward the CCP government on its political participation, I first assess the major forms of the middle class's political participation and their extent.

A. Major Forms of Political Activities and Their Frequencies

In democratic societies, the middle class is considered more likely than other social groups to participate in various forms of political activities, such as voting in elections at various levels. Participation by the middle class also is regarded as crucial for the maintenance and functioning of a democratic system (Dahl 1971; Lane 1959; Milbrath 1977). According to Sidney Verba and his associates, conventional forms of political activities are "legal acts by private citizens that are more or less directly aimed at influencing the selection of governmental personnel and the actions that they take" (Verba, Nie, and Kim 1978). Verba and his associates identify four *modes of conventional political participation*: voting, campaign activity, communal activity, and particularized contact. Following the insights from studies of political participation in the West, some China analysts have tried to define and identify conventional forms of political activities that the middle class as well as other social classes engage in. These scholars have identified several common modes of conventional political participation: voting, campaign behavior, particularized contact, and civic participation (Jennings 1997; Manion 1996; Shi 1997; Chen 2000, 2004).

Based on these extant studies of political participation engaged in by the middle class and the non-middle class, in both Chinese and non-Chinese settings, I designed a questionnaire for this study that consisted of seven questions concerning respondents' political behavior (Table 5.1). Furthermore, to identify major clusters or categories of political participation, I ran an exploratory factor analysis of all seven items, using the sample of middle-class respondents.[1] As the table shows, two major factors emerged from the factor analysis, each of which deals with a category of political participation: election participation and contacting/petitioning. Election participation involves voting in elections for community residents' committees (CRCs) and local people's congresses and participating

Table 5.1 Factor Analysis of Participation Items, Middle Class, China[a]

Item	Contacting and Petitioning	Election Participation
Petitioning government individually	.746	
Petitioning government collectively	.716	
Contacting party or government officials	.685	
Contacting representatives of local people's congress	.620	.348
Voting in CRC election		.813
Participating in CRC nomination		.653
Voting in local people's congress election		.581

[a] Figures are factor loadings of .25 or larger from the varimax rotated matrix for all factors with eigenvalues greater than 1.0.

in the nomination of candidates for CRCs. The category of contact-
ing/petitioning consists of contacting party or government officials,
contacting representatives of local people's congresses, and petitioning the government at various levels either collectively or individually. These two factors together explain about half (57.3%) of
the variance among the seven items. While the contacting/petition-
ing category explains 31.2% of the variance, the election participation category explains 16.2% of the variance. The factor scores for
these two categories are used as the indexes of the two categories
of political participation in the analysis that follows.

There are two major reasons to choose these two categories of
political participation for this study. One is that, although these
two categories do not exhaust all the political acts taken by the
Chinese middle class, they are the most common forms of political
behavior in China (Manion 1996; Shi 1997; Jennings 1997; Tang
and Parish 2000). Thus, they are most likely to represent the fundamental dimensions of the middle class's political participation. The
other reason is that because these acts are considered "legitimate in
China, at least in theory" (though certainly not risk-free), questions
about these acts are "unlikely to make respondents give interviewers false answers" (Shi 1997, 27). Consequently, the responses to
the questions in these two categories are expected to be truthful.

Table 5.2 shows the frequency of each of the seven political acts
in the two categories of political participation. In the election category, voting in the elections for local people's congresses was the
most common political act performed by middle-class respondents.
Over 60% of these respondents had voted in the most recent elections for local people's congresses. By contrast, a far small percentage voted in CRC elections (17%), and participating in CRC
nominations was the lowest of all (5%).

In the contacting/petitioning category, the act of contacting
party or government officials and representatives of local people's
congresses was done more frequently by the middle-class respondents in our sample than were the remaining two participatory
forms (petitioning the government collectively and petitioning

Table 5.2 Frequency of Political Participation, Middle Class, China

Item	Number	Percent[a]
Election participation		
Voting in local people's congress election	410	60.47
Voting in CRC election	115	16.96
Participating in CRC nomination	31	4.57
Contacting and petitioning		
Contacting party or government officials	25	3.69
Contacting representatives of local people's congress	20	2.95
Petitioning government collectively	15	2.21
Petitioning government individually	7	1.03

[a] Percentages represent positive (yes) responses. $N = 736$.

the government individually). Specifically, within the year prior to our survey, a mere, 3–4% of respondents contacted party or government officials or representatives of people's congresses, while only 1–2% petitioned the government individually or collectively.

B. Distinction between the Two Categories of Political Activities

It is equally worth noting that as the results of the exploratory factor analysis of all seven items (i.e., the identification of two major factors) indicate, these two categories of political activity are distinct from one another. This empirical finding about the distinction between the two categories of political participation is consistent with a previous study of urban mass political participation in post-Mao China (see Chen 2004, chapter 6). Given the consistency of the findings between current and previous studies, this distinction can presumably be explained by the sociopolitical characteristics of each of the two participatory categories as explained below, characteristics that have been identified in the previous study (Chen 2004, chapter 6).

A close examination of these characteristics enables a better understanding of the middle class's political behavior.

Election Participation. In the late 1970s and early 1980s, the CCP under Deng Xiaoping amended the electoral law for the elections for people's congresses, or Chinese "legislatures," at various levels. This new law introduced direct elections for local people's congresses.[2] In theory, the new law allowed voters to nominate candidates and have a choice among multiple candidates for each contested seat. Of all seven forms of political participation examined in this study, voting in these elections has been the most common political act of urban citizens. As Table 5.2 demonstasted, over 60% of our middle-class respondents voted in the most recent elections for local people's congresses. Thus, we need to pay closer attention to this type of political behavior by examining political/structural constraints on and citizens' choices in these elections, as well as the political role of the local people's congresses themselves.

First, consider the political/structural constraints on the elections, which have been determined mainly by the CCP. The fundamental motive of the CCP leadership to introduce and maintain the new electoral law has been twofold. First and foremost, the CCP leadership intended to regain and reinforce the legitimacy of its one-party rule through liberalized yet limited local elections (e.g., O'Brien 1990, 126; McCormick 1996, 31). By allowing people to elect deputies *directly* to the lowest level of people's congresses, the post-Mao leaders expected to create an image of the government's "representativeness" among the citizens (McCormick 1996). Second, and *only second*, these electoral reforms were also intended to heighten the efficiency of the government (O'Brien 1990, 126), as the "popularly" elected deputies would, ideally, act on behalf of their constituents to advocate sensible policies and block unpopular governmental decisions at various legislative levels. How well this second objective has been achieved through local elections remains questionable. But it must be noted that since the outset of the electoral reforms, the CCP leaders have always linked this objective to their ultimate political goal: strengthening the legitimacy of the "party leadership" (*dang de lingdao*) (see, e.g., Archive Research Office 1994, chapter 10). In short, it is very clear that all these limited electoral reforms were mainly *intended* by the CCP to strengthen its own legitimacy by improving its capacity to govern rather than to initiate democratic competition across political and ideological divides.

From this fundamental motive, the CCP leaders—from Deng Xiaoping to Jiang Zeming and Hu Jintao—have firmly imposed at least two formidable constraints on the local people's congress elections. One is political. To prevent any organized and individual opposition from challenging its position of absolute rule, the CCP has directly or indirectly controlled virtually the entire process of local people's congress elections, from the nomination of candidates, to electorate deliberation, to the determination of final candidates on the ballot (Halpern 1991, 38; Burns 1999, 591). This political control has been executed mainly by the party-dominated local election committees (Shi and Lei 1999, 21–23). These committees also control the final results of the elections via a procedure labeled the "three ups and three downs,"[3] in which local party leaderships eventually get the voters' "consent" for the final candidates placed on the ballot— most of whom are either party members or at least obedient to the party line (McCormick 1996). Furthermore, no candidates representing opposition or even independent parties or organizations are allowed in these elections. The so-called democratic parties that have long been co-opted by the CCP may participate, but their participation serves only as window-dressing for China's so-called "democracy with Chinese characteristics." In her observation of recent elections for local people's congresses, Sharon LaFraniere (2011), a correspondent of the *New York Times*, confirmed that the CCP "authorities routinely [denied] voters the chance to freely choose a political representative" who was independent from the communist party.

The other constraint imposed by the CCP in these elections is an ideological one. The party has implemented a list of measures to prevent local people's congress elections from becoming a forum for spreading "bourgeois liberal thoughts" or political views contrary to the official ideology. First of all, the party prohibits any large-scale or "publicized" electoral campaigning because it is considered part of "bourgeois democracy" (as opposed to "social- ist democracy"), and it requires that all electoral activities and deliberations be carried out within a limited scope (e.g., work unit or *danwei*) under firm control by the party-dominated elec- tion committee (Wang 1998; Shi and Lei 1999, 23 and 28–30). By doing so, the CCP has almost eliminated any effective channels for potential dissidents to articulate their opinions in local elec- tions. Consequently, as McCormick observed, "with the excep- tion of a few isolated cases,... candidates [could not] campaign in the usual sense of that word," and they could typically give only a few-minute-long self-introduction, stating mainly that they were "the sort of persons recommended in the official guidelines" (McCormick 1996, 41).

Not only has the CCP severely restricted the scope and format of electoral activities and deliberations, but it has also made relentless efforts to control the substance of the activities and deliberations to make sure that no political view contrary to the CCP's "four car- dinal principles"[4] sneaks into the local elections. Especially since the inconvenient appearance of a few non-Marxist candidates (who strongly advocated some radical political views deviating from the party line) in the 1980 local elections (Halpern 1991, 46; O'Brien 1990, 129),[5] the CCP has instructed all electoral committees to watch and prevent any speeches "threatening the party's leader- ship" and the nation's "stability and unity" (Wang 1998, 279).

In short, "with scattered exceptions in 1979–1980," as Andrew Nathan (1997, 235) rightly concludes, local people's congress elec- tions so far "have not turned into competitive campaigns owing to tight party control." Thus, as mentioned earlier, the overwhelming net outcomes of these elections have been very much in accordance with the CCP's expectations. Politically, most of the winning can- didates are party members, none of them comes from any form of organized opposition, and none of them are independent candidates who operates without the party's support or approval. Ideologically, very few of the winning candidates advocate political views different from the party line, although some of them have made "constructive suggestions" on some specific local policy issues.

Second, to have a better understanding of voting in local people's congress elections as a form of political participation, we also need to ascertain what choices are available to voters in such elections. Despite the aforementioned political and ideological constraints, the current electoral system still offers voters two kinds of choices in local people's congress elections. One is that, as mentioned previously, voters can have alternative candidates (but only *within* the political and ideological constraints set by the CCP). In other words, while voters cannot nominate or vote for any candidates who challenge the fundamental norms and institutions of the political regime, they do have choices among the candidates who appear on the CCP-sanitized ballots. More important, the overwhelming majority of the final candidates on the ballots differ only in degree rather than in kind: they may differ in their opinions on some specific local policy issues or in their "popularity" among the voters.

The other choice available to voters is to abstain from the elections without penalty. While in pre-reform elections the people were coerced by the regime to vote (see, e.g., Townsend 1969), in today's partially reformed or semicompetitive elections, they are given a choice between voting and not voting. In other words, today's voters have the freedom of *non*-voting in the current elections. With this freedom, those who dislike the fundamental political and ideological orientations sanctioned by the party may choose not to vote as a form of protest. Conversely, those who support (or at least are indifferent to) the party's orientations tend to participate in these local elections by choice.

Third, we must understand the role that local congress deputies play in order to analyze people's motives for voting. According to the People's Republic of China (PRC) constitution, local people's congresses should play an important role in representing citizens' interests and supervising local governments and their officials.[6] In reality, however, the congresses and their deputies have by no means met these "expectations." Based on extensive field observation, for example, McCormick (1996, 42) has vividly described the local people's congresses' lack of either the means or the power to exercise constitutionally prescribed functions, as follows:

> Once elected, deputies...tend to disappear. The overwhelming majority of deputies whom I interviewed did not receive time off work other than to attend annual meetings and for one or two inspection tours per year. Nor did most deputies have any means for regular communication with their constituents.... Deputies are generally not allowed to speak from the floor to the whole congress. Nearly all of the time the whole house is in session is dominated by the local leadership reading lengthy work reports. The major work of most sessions of people's congresses is to approve these reports.... Deputies are encouraged to forward requests from their constituents to the government but these are also filtered through the leadership prior to reaching their targets.

In short, systemic political factors have prevented the local people's congresses and their deputies from playing a truly representative and legislative role. The local people's congresses therefore become more or less a facade of "democracy," which simply gives "substance to the Party's claim to have established a democracy" (McCormick 1996, 41).

An overall picture of local people's congress elections should be quite clear from what has been discussed thus far. On the one hand, local people's congress elections operate under two severe constraints, one political and the other ideological. On the other hand, these elections offer the electorate only two choices, both of which are limited: a choice among multiple, party-approved candidates for each position, and the choice to abstain from voting. These constraints and choices in the elections so far, I believe, have constituted fundamental rules of the game in the local people's congress elections. Furthermore, apparently, local people's congresses and their deputies have by and large fallen short of representing constituents' interests and overseeing the government. The limits placed upon the elected congresses and their deputies also influence voters' attitudes toward the elections themselves. Under these circumstances, how do the political attitudes toward democracy of the middle class affect its participation in elections? This question will be addressed in the discussion that follows.

Contacting/Petitioning Behavior. As mentioned earlier, this category of political participation consists of four specific political acts in this study: contacting party or government officials, contacting representatives of local people's congresses, and petitioning the government at various levels either collectively or individually. To have a better understanding of this category of participation, I attempt to address several important questions that concern the nature and structural setting of this category of political activity.

First of all, about what do people in China want to contact government officials at various levels? This category of political act can be regarded as "particularistic" in urban China (see Tang and Parish 2000, 187–199). By contacting government officials, people express their concerns about and interests in concrete personal and, sometimes, local community issues, such as employment, wages, housing, local pollution, welfare, education, medical care, community order, and local government corruption.

Second, why do people in China need to contact leaders at various levels through different channels to address these concrete issues? In their survey-based study of urban China, Tang and Parish (2000, 189) have argued that "the government still controls resource allocation and provides extensive social services in urban areas, such as employment, income, housing, education, and health care." Although such government controls have gradually declined since the post-Mao reforms began, most ordinary people, including those in the middle class, still depend on the government for a large part of their everyday needs. In this kind of structural setting, therefore, people who are not satisfied with the existing allocation of resources or services by the government may still feel the need to contact work unit leaders (for those employed in the state sector) or government officials (for those employed in the non-state sector) at various levels to seek desired changes in policies and regulations.

Third, how do people contact and voice their concerns to leaders at various levels? To achieve their personal and communal goals, people in urban areas may contact and voice their opinions to leaders in a number of ways. Based on his field observation, Shi (1997, 45) has summarized the various options used by ordinary people in urban areas:

> Some people choose to contact officials at the work unit level; others go to higher government organizations. Participants use various strategies when contacting government officials. Some people contact government officials in a conciliatory manner, to persuade government officials to make beneficiary decisions; others choose a confrontational style, to put pressure on the officials to induce desired changes. Still others contact government officials through patron-client ties, to turn the relationship from a hierarchical one into an exchange.

One's choice of strategy to contact leaders usually depends on one's employment status, his or her socioeconomic resources, and his or her purposes.

Compared to voting in local elections, however, this kind of political activity requires more initiative, determination, time, and communication skill. In addition, such an activity though considered legal, is not totally risk-free, as some targeted officials and agencies may perceive this kind of activity as challenges to their authority and hence retaliate against participants. Not everyone is willing and can afford to take such risks. In short, contacting officials and voicing concerns to them are certainly more demanding and riskier acts than is voting in local elections. In the sample, therefore, the number of respondents who engaged in these activities was much lower than that of those who voted in elections for local people's congresses.

To summarize, there are both distinctions and similarities between these two major categories of political participation, both of which have important implications for an analysis of the role of democratic support in shaping political behavior. First, one of the critical distinctions between these two categories lies in the potential outcomes that may result from participation. On the one hand, voting (or nonvoting) may produce spiritual gains[7] for voters, since elected congresses and deputies generally do not deliver concrete policy initiatives. Thus, this type of political behavior is more likely to be associated with one's political beliefs and values, such as support for democracy and support for the government. On the other hand, contacting leaders at various levels to complain about specific policies/regulations and officials/agencies could lead to particular material benefits for individuals. Thus, this type of political behavior is likely to be "unrelated to a person's beliefs about the larger political system" (Bahry and Silver 1990, 826); rather, it tends to be correlated with one's evaluation of incumbent policies.

Second, one of the most important commonalities between these two categories of political acts is that both types of acts are legitimate and, to a certain extent, encouraged by the government, although neither is totally risk-free. Consequently, people may exercise their free will to determine whether they should participate in these two forms of political activities. Thus, involvement in these activities may provide a reliable test of the relationship between support for democracy as a set of attitudes and a person's political behavior.

II. Impact of Democratic Support on Political Participation

In this study I assume that middle-class attitudes toward democracy and democratization may variably influence the two different categories of middle-class political participation. This difference in the impact of democratic support between the two behavioral categories results mainly from the distinctive natures of the two categories.

There are at least two distinct views about the impact of support for democracy on electoral behavior in China. One argues that the semidemocratic (vs. totalitarian or non-democratic) electoral system in China provides citizens with limited yet genuine opportunities to express their opinions and exert influence (Shi 1999a, 1999b). Therefore, those who support democratic values and institutions tend to engage in these elections in post-Mao China. In other words, people's support for democracy and democratization has a positive effect on their participation in government-sanctioned elections, such as the elections for local people's congresses.

The other view contends that attitudinal support for democracy has either a negative impact or no impact on formal and conventional forms of participation, such as voting in local people's congress elections (Chen 2000; Chen and Zhong 2002; Zhong and Chen 2002). According to this view, all of these formal and conventional channels of participation are *firmly* controlled by the party, and such tight control in turn alienates democratic supporters. Consequently, those who adhere to democratic values and institutions tend to see the formal and conventional channels as a formality, which "serves only the function of legitimizing the non-democratic, one-Party rule" (Zhong and Chen 2002, 185). As such, democratic supporters either ignore these channels or boycott them in protest against one-party rule.

From the contending views described here, one can derive two competing hypotheses concerning the impact of democratic support on the middle class's participation in formal electoral channels, such as the elections for local people's congresses and CRCs. One is that those members of the middle class who support democratic principles and institutions are less likely to participate in those elections, because they consider the elections non-democratic. The other hypothesis states, to the contrary, that democratic supporters tend to participate in these elections because elections may provide opportunities for political change. In the analysis that follows, we test these two competing hypotheses against the survey's sample of the middle-class respondents.

Similarly, there are also two contending views about the role of democratic support (or non-support) in shaping contacting/petitioning activities in non-democratic settings. One view is that democratic supporters are not likely to contact government officials or petition governments because they regard officials and governments as the products of a non-democratic political system (Chen 2000). The other view suggests that those who support democratic values and principles may indeed engage in contacting/petitioning activities in a non-democratic system, as they consider officials to be viable, potential channels for making incremental changes and expressing their opinions (Bahry and Silver 1990, 836). Based on these two views, two competing hypotheses can be developed: members of the middle class who support democratic values and institutions are either likely to contact officials and petition governments at various levels or they are unlikely to do so.

To explore these competing hypotheses, I ran two separate bivariate cross-tabulations. One investigated the correlation between democratic support and voting behavior; the other examined the relationship between such support and contacting/petitioning behavior. Table 5.3 presents the results of the correlation between democratic support and voting behavior. In general, these results indicate a significant, negative correlation between these two variables: those respondents who displayed a high level of democratic support were unlikely to participate in elections, while those who had a low level of democratic support had a high frequency of voting. For instance, most (60%) of those who were least supportive ("low") of democracy participated in elections most frequently ("high"), while more than half (52.2%) of those who were most supportive of democracy ("high") participated in elections least frequently ("low"). These results, therefore,

Table 5.3 Correlation Between Democratic Support and Voting Behavior

Frequency of Voting Activities	Level of Democratic Support		
	Low %	Medium %	High %
Low	7.5	14.0	52.2
Medium	33.4	41.5	20.2
High	59.1	44.5	27.6
TOTAL	100	100	100
	gamma = −.71*		

Note: All questionnaire items of the variable for democratic support and those of the variable for voting activities are combined to form two additive indexes, respectively: the level of democratic support and the frequency of voting activities. Then, each of these two indexes is trichotomized into three categories: high, intermediate, and low levels.
* $p < .05$.

Table 5.4 Correlation Between Democratic Support and Petitioning/Contacting Activities

Petitioning/Contacting Activities	Level of Democratic Support		
	Low %	Medium %	High %
Low	56.5	18.0	24.6
Medium	21.2	48.4	31.5
High	22.3	33.6	43.9
TOTAL	100	100	100
	gamma = .67*		

Note: All questionnaire items of the variable for democratic support and those of the variable for petitioning/contacting activities are combined to form two additive indexes, respectively: the level of democratic support and the frequency of petitioning/contacting activities. Then, each of these two indexes is trichotomized into three categories: high, intermediate, and low levels.
* $p < .05$.

support one of the competing hypotheses discussed previously: that is, those members of the middle class who support democratic principles and institutions are less likely to participate in the CCP-sanctioned elections.

The results of the bivariate correlation between democratic support and contacting/petitioning behavior among the middle-class respondents are shown in Table 5.4. The results indicated that among our middle-class respondents, those who strongly supported democracy and democratization seemed mostly likely to participate in petitioning and contacting activities, while those who were less in favor of democracy tended to be least likely to participate in such activities. For instance, about 44% of those who registered a high level of democratic support also engaged in a higher frequency of participation/contacting activities, while a majority (57%) of those who had a low level of support for democracy had a low level of participation in these activities. These results apparently support one of the two competing propositions mentioned earlier: that is, members of the middle class who believe in democratic values and institutions are likely to contact officials and petition governments at various levels.

The results of the bivariate analyses of the correlations between democratic support and the two types of political participation, presented in Tables 5.3 and 5.4, will be further verified through the more robust tests of multivariate analyses that follow. I now turn to another important cause of political participation within the middle class, employment in the state sector.

III. Impact of State-Sector (Versus Non-State-Sector) Employment on Political Participation

As I have discussed in the previous chapters, employment status and work settings may influence people's political attitudes. I have also found that those members of the middle class employed in the state sector tend to be less supportive of political change toward democracy, because such a change may threaten the current state and therefore jeopardize their vested interests. Similarly, it may also be assumed that within the middle class, those working in the state sector tend to be less likely than those in non-state sector to participate in political activities that may be considered more likely to challenge the state and so be detrimental to their individual well-being. This is simply because the middle-class members who are employed in the state sector lack an incentive to challenge the state, with which they have stronger ideational, institutional, and material ties. Consider urban housing conditions as an example to illustrate the difference between the state-sector and non-state-sector members of the middle class in their motivations for political participation.

Prior to the post-Mao reform, urban residents did not own their apartments. Almost all the housing facilities were owned by the government, which "distributed" them to almost all urban residents at a low rent (Whyte 1985; Tang and Parish 2000; Zhou 2004). Since the early 1980s, the Chinese government has gradually privatized housing and eventually stopped distributing housing in urban areas (Wang and Murie 1996; Chiu 2001). As a result, all urban residents have to purchase their own apartments either through their work units (in the case of those employed in the state sector) at subsidized rates or through the market (in the case of those employed in the non-state sector) at higher, market rates. Consequently, the privatization of housing created two types of home ownerships: commercial housing (*shangping fang*) ownership and work unit–subsidized housing (*danwei fuli fang*) ownership. Usually, middle-class people in the non-state sector has commercial housing ownership, while those in the state sector enjoy work-unit–subsidized housing ownership (Chiu 2001; Read 2004; Tomba 2004).

Like their Western counterparts, members of China's middle class are generally very much interested in protecting their private property, such as their homes. But the two subgroups—in the state sector and in the non-state sector—of the middle class in China may react *differently* to issues that negatively affect their real estate. The state-sector middle class tends to contact their work units through conventional and institutionalized, but less challenging, channels to resolve issues. This behavior perhaps reflects the underlying fact that this group has close institutional and ideational ties with the party-state. But the non-state-sector middle class tends to resort to less conventional and institutional, and more authority-challenging, measures, such as petitioning the government individually or collectively and contacting party or government officials.

The demands of the non-state-sector middle class have posed some challenges to the authorities, at least at the local levels. Politically competent and knowledgeable middle-class people in the private sector have taken unconventional actions, such as forming homeowners' associations and organizing protests to defend their property interests and rights (Read 2004; Tomba 2004; Cai 2005). Some empirical studies and reports have documented the role of newly emerging homeowners' associations in helping non-state-sector middle-class individuals protect their interests (Dolven 2003; Fan 2005; Read 2004). It should be noted here that homeowners' associations are, on many occasions, initiated and self-managed by the residents. However, in many urban areas, the local governments have not recognized the legitimacy of these associations and have restricted their activities.[8] Furthermore, when their demands cannot be met, competent non-state-sector middle-class individuals may even go on to organize protests and demonstrations.

Many earlier studies have documented collective acts perpetrated by members of the non-state-sector middle class in defense of their property rights (Cai 2005; Read 2004). For instance, the non-state-sector middle class has organized homeowners' associations to bargain collectively with the government and real estate companies (Cai 2005; Read 2004). As one of the interviewees, Mrs. 118, said in an in-depth interview with her:

We spent our own money buying our apartments. The government cannot impinge on our interests at its own wish. If that happens, we have no other choice but to organize ourselves and negotiate with the government collectively.

The Iron Tower (*tie ta*) Rights Protection campaign of 2005 is a good example of self-interest protection by the non-state-sector middle class. In this case, residents of the *Hui'long'guan* community in Beijing's *Changping* district, most of whom were young intellectuals and businesspeople from the private sector, launched this Rights Protection campaign to protect their rights of ownership of their apartments. Their local government wanted to construct a telecom building close to the *Hui'long'guan* community. Residents of the *Hui'long'guan* community believed that the electromagnetic radiation of the telecom building's antennae could impair their health; thus, they strongly opposed the construction of this building. Beginning around 2005, incidents related to property rights protection increased in large and medium-sized cities. In addition to organizing homeowners' associations, owners of commercial apartments, most of whom are members of the non-state-sector middle class, engaged in other activities to protect their property, such as collecting signatures through Internet forums and calling for a more democratic decision-making process in the management of residential community affairs (Cai 2005; Dolven 2003).

All in all, from these activities to protect property rights in urban China, at least two key lessons can be drawn about the differences in political behavior that distinguish the two subgroups of the middle class in contemporary China. One is that while both state-sector and non-state-sector groups of the middle class may share many common interests—such as protection of individual rights and private property and maintenance of the general sociopolitical status quo—they may pursue these interests in different ways due to their differential relationships to the party-state. The other lesson is that because the ideational and institutional ties with the party-state of the non-state-sector group are weaker than those of the state-sector group, the former tends to choose less conventional and more authority-challenging styles of political participation than does the state-sector group. These lessons suggest that the non-state-sector group of the middle class should be more likely to participate in "contacting and petitioning" activities, which are considered less conventional and more authority challenging than the "election participation" activities.

To explore this expectation, I ran two separate bivariate analyses of the correlations through two cross-tabulations. One of the analyses was designed to explore the correlation between employment status and election participation, while the other dealt with the link between that status and contacting/petitioning behavior. Table 5.5 shows the results of the correlation between employment status and election participation. Overall, the results seem to be supportive of the expectation: that is, those middle-class individuals who were employed in the state sector were more likely to participate in voting activities than were those employed in the non-state sector. Specifically, a majority (54%) of those in the state sector enjoyed a high frequency of participation in elections, while most (63%) of those in the non-state sector engaged in little or none of the election activities.

The results from the bivariate analysis dealing with the correlation between employment status and contacting/petitioning activities appear in Table 5.6. These results also are consistent with

Table 5.5 Correlation Between Employment Status and Voting Behavior

Voting Behavior	Employment Status	
	Non-state Sector %	**State Sector %**
Low	62.5	13.6
Medium	18.1	33.1
High	19.4	53.9
TOTAL	100	100
	gamma = .75*	

Note: All questionnaire items of the variable for voting behavior are combined to form an additive index, the frequency of voting behavior. Then, this index is trichotomized into three categories: high, intermediate, and low levels. Employment in the state apparatus = 1; employment outside of the state apparatus = 0.
* $p < .05$.

my earlier expectation: those in the non-state sector participate more actively in contacting/petitioning activities than do those in the state sector. For instance, a majority (73%) of those in the non-state sector reported a medium or high level of engagement in contacting/petitioning activities, while only about 30% of those employed in the state sector had the same level of engagement.

IV. The Multivariate Analyses

I have thus far presented the results of the *bivariate* analyses of the correlations between the middle class's attitudes toward democracy and its employment status on the one hand, and its participation in the two categories of political activities, on the other. However, *multivariate* analyses, which can provide a more robust test of each causal relationship, are needed to determine the independent effect of each of our explanatory variables on the middle class's political behavior. For that purpose, I ran two multiple regression models (OLS) using the sample of middle-class respondents from this survey.[9] One

Table 5.6 Correlation Between Employment Status and Contacting/Petitioning Behavior

Contacting/Petitioning Behavior	Employment Status	
	Non-state Sector %	State Sector %
Low	26.5	70.1
Medium	27.2	17.2
High	46.3	12.7
TOTAL	100	100
	gamma = −.71*	

Note: All questionnaire items of the variable for voting behavior are combined to form an additive index, the frequency of voting behavior. Then, this index is trichotomized into three categories: high, intermediate, and low levels. Employment in the state apparatus = 1; employment outside of the state apparatus = 0.
* $p < .05$.

Table 5.7 Multiple Regressions (OLS) of Political Participation by Democratic Support within the Middle Class[a]

	Electoral Category (Model 1)[b]	Contacting/ Petitioning Category (Model 2)[c]
Democratic support[d]	−.080* (.041)	0.110** (0.043)
Employment in the state apparatus[e]	.077* (.048)	−0.080* (0.043)
Sex[f]	−.006 (.076)	−0.027 (0.079)
Age	.018** (.004)	0.061* (0.005)
Education[g]	−.038 (.047)	0.064 (0.050)
Household gross income[h]	−.115 (.074)	−0.170** (0.077)
Party membership[i]	.231** (.094)	0.093 (0.107)
Location[j]		
Beijing	.432** (.102)	0.156 (0.107)
Chengdu	.603** (.111)	0.174 (0.116)
Summary statistic constant	.295 (.768)	1.102 (0.803)
R^2	.261	.256
Adjusted R^2	.248	.238
N	678	678

*$p < .05$, ** $p < .01$.

[a] Standard errors are in parentheses.

[b] The value of electoral participation is the factor score of three items: participation in CRC election, participation in CRC nomination, and voting in local people's congress election.

[c] The value of contacting/petitioning is the factor score of four items: petitioning government individually, petitioning government collectively, contacting party or government officials, and contacting representatives of local people's congress.

[d] The value of support for democratic values and institutions is the factor score of the four dimensions: support for participatory norm, valuation of political liberty (vs. order), support for competitive election, and rights consciousness.

[e] The state apparatus includes government and party agencies, state-owned enterprises, and public organizations. Employment in the state apparatus = 1; employment outside of the state apparatus = 0.

[f] Male = 1; female = 2.

[g] Middle school and below = 1; high school = 2; post-secondary professional training = 3; four-year university education = 4; graduate school = 5.

[h] Household income = natural log (gross household income).

[i] Non-party member = 0; party member = 1.

[j] Xi'an is set as a reference group.

model is for election participation; the other is for contacting/petitioning activities (Table 5.7). In each of these models, I also included three types of control variables to ascertain whether the middle class's attitudes toward democracy and its employment status each independently influences its political behavior. These three categories of factors are: a person's affiliation with the state apparatus, his or her key sociodemographic attributes, and the socioeconomic conditions of the area where the person resides.

Overall, the two regression models indicate that attitudinal orientations toward democratic values and institutions—the independent variable in both models—significantly and negatively affect the middle class's participation in elections (model 1), but significantly and positively influence the middle class's involvement in contacting and petitioning activities (model 2). The impact of democratic support on both kinds of political behavior is independent of the control variables. In other words, those in the middle class who strongly support democratic values and institutions are not likely to participate in elections for local people's congresses and CRCs but are likely to contact government officials and government institutions individually or collectively.

These findings appear to support two of the four hypotheses mentioned earlier. One of them is that those who support democratic values and institutions tend to see the formal and conventional channels—such as local elections for people's congresses and CRCs—as a formality, which "serves only the function of legitimizing the non-democratic, one-Party rule" (Chen and Zhong 2002, 185). Democratic supporters thus either ignore these channels or boycott them in protest against one-party rule.

As an example, consider an interview with a financial manager of a joint venture company in Beijing, Mr. 10. This respondent believed in democratic values and was very critical of the current local elections for people's congresses and CRCs. In an interview, he said:

> The current local election of people's congresses is only semi-democratic. Nomination of candidates is virtually controlled

by local party and government offices. According to the constitution, all political parties—including other parties than the Communist Party—and social organizations may either jointly or separately recommend candidates for people's congress; any voter or people's deputy (to local people's congresses) may also nominate a candidate with an endorsement by at least ten people. However, this is not the case in practice. It is very difficult for any voter or people's deputy to recommend a candidate, because of the tight control by the party. In addition, direct election of people's deputies is limited only to the local people's congress (county level and township level). Above this level, all deputies to people's congresses are indirectly elected. Such indirect elections give the party lots of opportunities to exert its political control. Third, political competition in the local election of people's congresses is very limited or non-existent. There are very few organized political campaigns, and almost no direct interactions between candidates and voters. As a result, most voters do not know the candidates before the election day. In my opinion, the current local election for people's congresses is only a pretention to so-called socialist democracy; it has no real meaning.

He continued to talk about elections for CRCs in urban areas:

As for the election of Community Residential Committee members, there is no importance at all. What do these committees do? The community residential committee only does minor things in [the] community. The real power of community management is in the hands of [the] property management company. Much worse, the election per se is not democratic. For example, many communities fail to hold direct elections of committee members; many don't adopt indirect elections for selecting committee members. Even worse, the nomination of candidates is controlled by street office (*jiedao*) leaders.

The other hypothesis the findings have substantiated is that those who support democracy (it should be stated, as a caveat, that the number of these democratic supporters among the middle-class respondents is small) may engage in contacting/petitioning activities. They prefer exercising influence this way, as they consider governments and individual officials at various levels—instead of the formal political procedures, such as local elections—to be meaningful channels through which they might be able to make incremental changes and, at least, express their opinions.

For example, an interview with a sales manager of a private firm in Chengdu, Mr 29, vividly illustrates the causal mechanisms between support for democracy and participation in contacting and petitioning activities. Mr. 29, who was in his mid-thirties, told us that:

The formal institutions have no real meaning in China, even though all these institutions claim to serve the interests of the people under the banner of socialist democracy. But I have to admit that there are some opportunities for us to voice our feelings about some issues, particularly non-political matters, under the current political setting, which is more open than that under Mao. When the issue is related to people's personal interests, at least some government officials are willing to solve the problem not by force but by negotiation. Sometimes and on some non-political issues, the government does encourage ordinary citizens to voice their interests by petitioning. So you may find that contacting government officials can be a very useful means to solve your problem. That seems to be a sign of improvement in the Chinese political system. That's why I have always tried to contact local officials for some issues about which I am concerned, such as lighting and the noise level in our neighborhood. Apparently, our contacts, along with those of others, have worked: the situation in our neighborhood has improved noticeably. I think all Chinese citizens should stand up and voice their interests through petitions. This is the only way that we can improve [the] Chinese political system and make it democratic.

As shown in Table 5.7, employment in the state apparatus has a positive impact on election participation but exerts a negative one on contacting and petitioning activities. These results suggest that those employed in the state apparatus are likely to participate in government-sanctioned elections, such as those for local people's congresses and for CRCs, but are unlikely to contact officials (outside of their own government agencies or state-owned enterprises) or to petition governments. To the contrary, those employed in the private sector tend to directly contact and petition government officials at various levels. These results confirm our earlier expectation that those in the non-state-sector group of the middle class are more likely to participate in contacting and petitioning activities, which are considered less conventional and more authority challenging than is participation in elections.

In terms of the sociodemographic attributes (which are control variables in these multivariate analyses), sex and education do not meaningfully influence either of the two categories of political action. However, age, income, and party membership variably affect one or both of them. Specifically, the older the respondents are, the more likely they are to participate in activities of both categories. Income does not significantly affect behavior in elections, but it does significantly, negatively influence involvement in contacting and petitioning activities. Those who have higher incomes are much less likely to contact officials or to petition governments. Moreover, party membership has a significant and positive impact on participation in elections, but it does not have a significant impact on contacting and petitioning activities.

Finally, the results from these two multivariate analyses are mixed when it comes to the impact of local socioeconomic conditions on political behavior. As indicated in Table 5.7, those who live in more developed areas (Beijing and Chengdu) are more likely to vote in local elections than those who live in a less developed area (Xi'an). But location of residence is not significantly associated with the middle class's contacting/petitioning activities.

V. Discussion and Conclusion

What are the patterns and frequency of political participation by China's middle class? How do the attitudes of China's new middle class toward democracy affect its political behavior? The findings in this chapter attempt to shed light on these questions. First of all, I have identified two main categories of political activity in which our middle-class respondents typically engage: election participation and contacting/petitioning. While these two categories are conceptually and empirically distinct, both are considered legitimate, though not completely risk-free, in contemporary China.

I have also found that election activities were more commonly practiced by middle-class respondents than were contacting and petitioning activities. It should be noted, however, that this study's empirical findings concerning the level of participation in these two categories of political activities by the middle-class respondents may not be generalized directly to China in its entirety, as they are derived from a survey of just three major cities. Nonetheless, they can help establish some needed statistical baselines about the level and characteristics of political participation by China's middle class, against which findings from other areas of the country can be compared.

As for the impact of the middle class's attitudes toward democracy on its political behavior, I have found that, while those who strongly support democratic values and institutions tend to stay away from the voting booth, they do tend to engage in activities

such as contacting individual officials and petitioning governments individually or collectively at various levels. In other words,
although most members of the middle class in China do not seem
to support democracy, those who do support it tend to ignore local
elections in favor of direct contacting and petitioning. In addition,
those employed in the state sector are more likely to participate in
conventional political activities, such as voting in elections, than
are those employed in the non-state sector; the latter group is more
likely to engage in less conventional (or more authority-challenging)
activities, such as contacting and petitioning government officials,
as compared with the former group.

What are the political implications of these findings? On the one
hand, the findings imply that China's formal political institutions—
such as elections for local people's congresses and CRCs—do not
seem to provide middle-class democratic supporters with desira-
ble channels to express their political preferences. On the other
hand, these democratic supporters, who represent just a minority of the middle class, do find informal political channels—such
as contacting officials and petitioning governments individually
or collectively—more meaningful ways to register their views and
demands. Consequently, one may conclude that, while the formal
channels of political participation tend to solicit support for the
current political system but discourage demands for democratic
change, the informal channels tend to facilitate a democratic tendency among the middle class. An increase by the middle class
in participating in informal channels, therefore, may presage a
larger role for the middle class as the agent of democratic change
in China.

6

Conclusion: Contingent Democratic Supporters and Prospects for Democracy

DOES THE MIDDLE class usually, if not always, support democracy and democratization in late-developing countries such as China? As indicated in chapter 1, this question has perplexed yet fascinated social scientists and policy makers alike for a number of decades. After World War II, a host of developing areas and countries acquired their independent statehoods and subsequently embarked economic development. Ever since, pundits of development have continuously speculated about the role of the middle class in political change, as well as economic development of these newly independent countries, most of which were "undemocratic" (Rose, Mishler, and Munro 2011, 157). For example, in his iconic portrayal and skillful analysis of what he labeled the "third wave" of democratization at the global level in the late twentieth century, a world-renowned political scientist, Samuel P. Huntington pointed out that one of the most powerful factors that helped bring about this wave of democratic transitions was the "greatly expended...urban middle class in many countries" (Huntington 1991, 45). The most recent popular uprisings against authoritarian regimes in the Arab world, in which the urban middle classes were said to have played a critical role, again served as an outstanding reminder of how the middle class can help to shape the course of political development in developing countries across cultural and geographical divides. This episode reveals the urgency of gaining a better grasp of this critical role.

Based on data collected from my probability-sample survey and in-depth interviews, all of which were conducted in major cities of China—Beijing, Chengdu, and Xi'an—between 2007 and 2008, I have sought to answer this fundamental question regarding the role of the middle class in democratization in the developing world. China is somewhat distinct from many other late-developing countries because, for example, of its robust one-party rule under the CCP and of the fact that its population is the largest in the world. As a late-developing country, however, China shares many features with other late- or late-late-developing countries. These include the stronger role of the state in economic development (compared to the roles of the states in early-industrializing countries), the recent emergence and growth of a new middle class, a strong connection between this class and the state, and the undemocratic nature of the state. Because of these similarities, the analyses presented in this book may be able to provide important lessons for our understanding of the political trajectory of the developing world, as well as the prospects for political change in China, in light of the middle class's attitudinal and behavioral orientations toward democracy and democratization.

To reinforce what has been discussed in the previous chapters on the Chinese middle class's attitudinal and behavioral orientations toward democracy, and to better understand the implications of what has been discussed for China and for the developing world, in this chapter, I will first recapitulate the general theoretical debates pertinent to the role of the middle class in democratization. I will then highlight empirical findings from this study and elucidate the key political and theoretical implications.

I. Theoretical Frameworks: Modernization, the Middle Class, and Democratization

The theoretical debates on the role of the middle class in democratization can be further understood in the broader context of the relationship between economic development and political democratization. The relationship—or causality—between development and democratization has been contemplated by generations of development analysts and political leaders in both developing and developed countries. While there has not been a clear and conclusive consensus about the nature and direction of the correlation between development and democracy, conventional wisdom among most development analysts and political leaders has seemed to tilt toward an idea that development leads to democratization. As Diane E. Davis (2004, 343–344) rightly pointed out,

> [T]he idea that development somewhat correlates with democracy is one of those claims that seems to circulate and recalculate in development circles. In our rapidly liberalizing world, this idea has produced a new generation of advocates, not just among U.S. State Department spokespeople but also within the halls of academe, so much so that it almost seems to have reached the status of a truism.

Furthermore, it should be noted that this implicit yet powerful "truism" has also been trapped within a seemingly cohesive framework that was explained in its purest sense, arguably, by Walt W. Rostow (1960) in his seminal work published in 1960, *The Stages of Economic Growth: A Non-Communist Manifesto*. Based on the experiences of Western Europe and North America, that framework posits that economically, all nations go through the same or similar sequential stages of economic development (i.e., the preconditions for takeoff, the takeoff, the drive to maturity, the age of high mass consumption, and the post-industrial age) to achieve their highest level of modernity. In addition, this framework predicts that politically and socially, a democratic system and greater justice inevitably result from these economic transformations. This theoretical proposition of the positive causal relationship between economic development and democracy was originally illustrated and substantiated by Seymour Martin Lipset (1959), who suggested that development leads to an increase in education, which in turn promotes political attitudes (e.g., general trust and political tolerance) conducive to democracy.

Consistent with this framework of modernization theory, many in the academe and policy-making circles believe that the middle class, as one of the most important products of economic development in modern times, serves as the most powerful catalyst of political democratization. This line of thinking, referred to in this book as the "unilinear approach," has embodied and reinforced the general framework of modernization theory by asserting the inevitability of the middle class's support for democracy and its catalytic role in democratization. In a nutshell, this approach assumes that there is a linear and sequential relationship among economic development, the emergence of the middle class, and political democratization. It contends that as modernization unfolds through the sequential stages— more or less similar to what Rostow describes—in a society, "economic development alters the pyramid-shaped social stratification system, in which the majority of the population is lower class and poor, to a diamond shape, in which the majority of the population is middle class and relatively well-off" (Muller 1997, 134). Subsequently, the middle class, out of self-interest, almost universally serves as the harbinger of democratization in a non-democratic society.[1] Specifically, the middle class supports a democratic system, because only in democracy can their individual rights and modest property holdings best be protected from potential encroachment by the government and the upper class (Glassman 1995, 1997). In addition, some of these scholars contend from the sociobehavioral perspective that middle-class individuals tend to favor democracy because, compared to the lower class, they have enough education and leisure time to enable them to understand and participate in public affairs effectively (Mills 1953; Lane 1959). This approach, which has been popularized by Lipset (1959, 1981) in his seminal work, *Political Man*, published in the late 1950s, has "resuscitated throughout subsequent decades in both quantitative study and political deliberation" (Davis 2004, 344).

As discussed in the previous chapters, however, there has been a serious challenge to this conventional wisdom. Perhaps this challenge has so far been more widely circulated in the academe than in the policy-making circles. As one of the earliest scholars leading the challenge, Alexander Gerschenkron (1962) criticized the core framework of modernization theory. Based on his examination and comparison of development experiences of several countries in Europe, he contends that modernization does not follow the same, linear path across countries, as modernization theory posits; instead, modernization may unfold in significantly different ways in early industrializers (such as the United Kingdom), late industrializers (such as Germany), and "late-late" industrializers (such as Russia) due to the distinct domestic and international conditions that each of these countries faces at a time.

This contending argument made by Gerschenkron against modernization theory has given rise to subsequent criticisms of the core framework of modernization theory. One of the most recent examples of such criticisms, which is also quite relevant to this study of a late-developing, non-democratic country, is the work of Valerie Bunce, Michael McFaul, and Kathryn Stoner-Weiss (2010). Based on their study of the most recent political changes in post-communist Europe and Eurasia, these analysts suggest that because of nations' various socioeconomic and sociopolitical conditions, modernization or development does not necessarily lead to a "cross-national spread of democratic orders"; instead, it sometimes is followed by dictatorship. In other words, according to this contending argument, there is not necessarily a causal, linear link between modernization and democratization.

In agreement with this view of the dynamic relationship between development and democratization, which directly challenges modernization theory, a group of analysts have developed an approach, regarded as the "contingent approach" in this study, to the role of the middle class in democratization during the course of modernization in late- or late-late-developing countries. The contingent approach suggests that the orientation of the middle class toward democracy is contingent upon some salient sociopolitical and socioeconomic conditions. These conditions vary with the sociopolitical context of each country and with the current economic development stage within each country. As discussed in the previous chapters, such conditions or factors include, but are not limited to, the middle class's dependence on (or independence from) the state, its perceived socioeconomic well-being, its political alliance with other classes (e.g., upper or working classes), its own class cohesiveness (or fragmentation), and its fear of political instability. As Rueschemeyer, Stephens, and Stephens (1992) suggest, for example, the role of the middle class in democratization can be ambiguous and will depend on its position in the class structure. In short, in the dynamic process of modernization as described by Gerschenkron and his followers, the middle class's orientation toward and its role in democratization is contingent upon critical socioeconomic and sociopolitical conditions surrounding that class in a certain society and at a given time.

In summary, the two major philosophical, theoretical traditions—modernization theory (popularized by Rostow and his followers) and its non-Marxian contender (powered by Gerschenkron and his believers)—posit two distinct relationships between economic development and democratization.

While modernization theory argues for a linear, positive link between development and democracy, its contender advocates for a non-linear, dynamic relationship between these two phenomena. Within each of these two theoretical camps, one distinct approach to the role of the middle class thrives. Rooted in modernization theory, the "unilinear approach" suggests that the middle class, as a product of modernization, inevitably promotes democratization; derived from the contender against modernization theory, the "contingent approach" contends that the orientation of this class toward democracy is dependent upon the specific socioeconomic and sociopolitical conditions in given societies.

Our findings here have provided empirical evidence that strongly supports the contingent approach while undermining the unilinear approach. To go even further, the findings have at least indirectly challenged modernization theory by suggesting that economic development does not inevitably produce a middle class that is supportive of democracy, and development does not inevitably bring about a democratic political system. To reinforce this conclusion, below I will highlight my key findings.

II. Empirical Findings: The Middle Class's Support for Democracy and Regime and Its Political Behavior

Throughout this book, I have sought to answer four fundamental questions: (1) Who constitutes the middle class in today's China? (2) Does this class support democracy or the current regime as the best form of government? (3) Why does or does not the middle class support democracy? (4) What impact does attitudinal orientation toward democracy have on the middle class's political behavior? The empirical evidence used to answer these questions comes mainly from data collected in a probability-sample survey and from in-depth interviews conducted in three major cities in China—Beijing, Chengdu, and Xi'an—in 2007 and 2008.

As explained in the first chapter, while the descriptive findings—particularly those about the proportion of the middle class in the population of the three cities, the levels of the middle class's support for democracy and for the incumbent government, and the magnitude of its participation in various political activities—may not be generalized *directly* to other parts of the developing world or other parts of China, these findings have provided critical baselines against which descriptive findings from future studies can be evaluated. The accumulation of these descriptive findings, accompanied by a continuing assessment of them, can eventually provide a more complete picture across regions of how much and in what sociopolitical and socioeconomic contexts middle-class citizens in other late developing countries around the world support democracy and democratization.

On the other hand, however, the relational findings presented in this book—particularly those about the impact of the key independent variables (e.g., the middle class's dependence on the state and its relatively high level of life satisfaction) on this class's support for democracy and for the government—can be directly applied to other parts of China, as well as to the developing world, especially to those settings where conditions resemble today's urban China. These findings explain the causal effects of the independent variables on the middle class's attitudinal and behavioral orientations toward democracy, as well as their stance toward the current undemocratic government.

In short, I argued that the findings from the data collected in the three Chinese cities and their implications can contribute to a well-informed reply to the four important questions posed above concerning middle-class people's attitudinal and behavioral orientations toward democracy. In this section, I highlight the empirical findings in the previous chapters.

A. Who Is the Middle Class in Today's China?

To operationalize the new middle class in China, which has emerged as a new social class and quickly expanded in size since the early 1990s, I have examined three types of measurement of the middle class (i.e., the subjective approach, the quantitative branch of the objective approach, and the qualitative branch of the objective approach), which are commonly used in the Western social science literature, in order to assess their applicability to Chinese society. My assessment is that the qualitative branch of the objective approach is most applicable to the study of the middle class in today's China.

First, as I argued in chapter 2, the subjective approach to identifying the middle class is not applicable to the Chinese setting. There are two fundamental reasons for my argument: first of all, the subjective approach requires that most of the population in a society have at least a basic understanding of what the middle class is (vs. other classes, such as the working class and the upper class), an understanding that can take a long time to develop. On the other hand, the Chinese people's subjective conceptualization of the middle class, however, is still far from congealing, even though the objective bases of class difference have formed since the onset of the post-Mao reform. For instance, a renowned sociologist from the Chinese Academy of Social Sciences, Chunling Li (2003), found that many Chinese people still do not acknowledge the appropriateness of the concept of class in Chinese society and only a few of them have grasped the meaning of social class and the criteria by which to identify different social classes.

Second, I do not believe that the quantitative branch of the objective approach is applicable to Chinese society. I have found that the level of income, the pivotal indicator commonly used in the quantitative branch of the objective approach, is not valid for the purpose of identifying the middle class in Chinese society. This is true because it is very hard to achieve a consensus on and consistency for the criterion of income when defining the middle class, since (1) an accurate account of personal income is hard to obtain and (2) income varies dramatically across the different regions of the country. More important, income does not necessarily indicate a person's true socioeconomic status in contemporary Chinese society (Chen 2004).

Finally, in light of these considerations, I have argued that the qualitative branch of the objective approach, which is based mainly on one's occupation, is the most suitable measurement of the middle class in contemporary China. As discussed earlier in this book, this measurement can overcome the drawbacks of the other two types of measurement. This is mainly because, in contemporary China, occupations are much easier to identify and more constant across regions than is personal income, and they tend to represent "groupings that are distinct and separate from one another" (Oppenheimer 1985, 7). Therefore, an occupation-based measurement is a more reliable and practical indicator of the middle class in Chinese society. Based on this occupation-based measurement, I have operationalized the middle class in China by combining four occupational groups typically considered to constitute the middle class in Western societies: self-employed laborers (*ge'ti'hu*), managerial personnel, professionals, and civil servants (*banshi renyuan*). The findings from the 2007–2008 survey indicate that at the time of the survey, the middle class, as defined by this occupation-based measurement, accounted for 24.4% of the population in Beijing, Chengdu, and Xi'an.

To gain a thorough understanding of the inherent sociopolitical attributes of China's new middle class, I have also examined the unique sociopolitical background in which this middle class emerged. The rise of the new middle class in contemporary China is a relatively new phenomenon and a direct consequence of the rapid state-led economic development over the past two decades. Therefore, the current middle class can be seen as the first generation of the new middle class in Chinese society. It could well be the

case that the class consciousness of the middle class has not yet
formed in China, since such a consciousness often takes more than
a generation to take shape.

Moreover, I have noted that the party-state has played a dominant role in creating and shaping this new middle class in contemporary China in the past two decades. In the course of this
process, a bifurcation arose between two subgroups within the
new middle class: a state-sector-based group and a non-state-
sector-based group. The state-sector group, as mentioned earlier, is employed by the state and accounts for more than half
(about 60%) of the middle class in today's urban China. That
group is composed primarily of managers in state-owned enterprises, professionals in public organizations, and staff members
in government and party agencies and in public organizations.
The non-state-sector group, though in the minority, has been
growing. This group includes managers in private and foreign-
invested enterprises, professionals in the non-state sector,
self-employed laborers, and white-collar office workers in the
non-state entities. While the emergence and growth of both subgroups of the new middle class have been heavily influenced by
the party-state's policies, it is definitely the state-sector group
that has been more dependent on and, accordingly, supportive of
the party-state than has been the non-state-sector group.

B. Does the Middle Class Support Democracy or the Current Regime in China?

I have examined both the levels of the middle class's support
for democracy and its support for the government, based on
data I have collected. First, to ascertain the extent of the middle class's support for a democratic political system, I have
examined middle-class people's attitudinal orientation toward
four categories of democratic values: (1) individual-rights
consciousness, (2) valuation of political liberty, (3) support

for participatory norms, and (4) support for competitive elections. The findings presented in the previous chapters demonstrate that while most members of the new middle class are in favor of individual rights, which are typically hailed and at least in theory protected in the democratic system, they are indifferent toward political liberties—such as the freedoms to demonstrate and to form organizations. They also are not interested in such democratic institutions as the fully competitive election of leaders without restriction on political parties, nor are they enthusiastic about participating in government affairs and politics. Moreover, the middle class is even less in favor of these democratic values and institutions than is the lower class.

Given the low level of support for democracy among the middle class, how strongly do its members support the current, undemocratic government led by the CCP? To answer this critical question that closely relates to the middle class's attitudes toward democratization, I have utilized a two-dimensional concept of political support to operationalize the support for the party-state by China's middle class, which encompasses diffuse support for the fundamental norms of the political regime and specific support for the major policies of the incumbent political authorities. The findings presented earlier have shown that, compared to the lower class, the middle class tends to be more supportive of the fundamental norms, values, and institutions of the current, undemocratic regime led by the CCP; it responds more favorably to the incumbent authorities' policies. More important, there is a strong, negative correlation between the middle class's support for the party-state and its support for democracy and democratization. In other words, those who support the party-state tend to be less likely to support political change toward a democratic system, since such a change would no doubt threaten the very existence of the undemocratic party-state.

C. Why Does or Does Not the Middle Class Support Democracy?

Why does or does not the middle class support democracy? To answer this crucial question, which is related to the role of the middle class in democratization, I have examined a set of sociopolitical factors that are considered to have influenced the middle class's attitudes toward democracy in China. I have found that the low level of the middle class's democratic support correlates with two categories of variables: (1) the middle class's ideational and institutional connections with the state (i.e., diffuse support and specific support for the party-state, fear of political instability that could be caused by further political reform, and employment/career dependence on the party-state), and (2) the middle class's assessment of its own economic and social statuses under the current party-state system. My findings lead me to conclude that most members of the new middle class in China apparently do not support democracy and democratization, largely due to their close and dependent relationship with the party-state, as well as because of their satisfaction with their own social and economic situation under the current regime. In other words, the attitudes of the new middle class toward democracy and democratization in today's China are linked to this class's ideational and material connection with the party-state.

In addition, it is worth noting that the results from the multivariate analysis presented in chapter 4 demonstrate that the two key categories of variables mentioned earlier exert a significant impact on the middle class's attitudinal orientation toward democracy, *independently* of several key sociodemographic factors, such as sex, education, income, party membership, and location. This finding suggests that the correlation between the two key categories of variables and the middle class's attitudes toward democracy is robust, transcending major demographic divides.

D. What Impacts Does Attitudinal Orientation Toward Democracy Have on the Middle Class's Political Behavior?

To assess the impact of attitudinal support for democracy on the middle class's political behavior, I have investigated middle-class people's participation in two kinds of political acts in urban China: (1) election participation, including voting in elections for local people's congresses and community residents' committees (CRCs) and getting involved in the nomination of candidates for CRCs, and (2) contacting/petitioning, which refers to contacting party and government officials or representatives of local people's congresses, and petitioning various levels of government collectively or individually. The findings show that among middle-class respondents, election participation was much more popular than was contacting/petitioning. For instance, a clear majority (over 60%) of middle-class respondents voted in the most recent elections for local people's congresses, even though these elections were firmly controlled by the CCP and utilized to legitimize the CCP's one-party rule.

The findings from our three-city survey indicated that while those who strongly supported democratic values and institutions tended to stay away from the voting booth in elections for local people's congresses and CRCs, they did tend to engage in activities such as contacting individual officials and petitioning governments. These results suggest that although most members of the middle class in China do not seem to support democracy, as indicated in this study, those who do support democracy are more likely to ignore local elections in favor of direct engagement in contacting and petitioning activities. These findings also imply that participating in elections may well be indicative of a lack of support for democracy but a presence of support for CCP rule, since the elections are firmly controlled by the CCP and utilized to legitimize its single-party rule.

Moreover, I have found that those employed in the state sector are more likely to participate in conventional political activities, such as voting in elections, than are those employed in the non-state sector. The non-state-sector group, on the other hand, is more likely to engage in unconventional (or more authority-challenging) activities, such as contacting and petitioning government officials, than is the state-sector group. These differences imply that while both state-sector and non-state-sector groups of the middle class may share common interests—such as a desire for protection of individual rights and private properties and for the maintenance of the socio-political status quo—they appear to pursue these interests in different ways, in accord with the proximity of their relationship to the party-state. These differences also seem to mean that because ideational and institutional bonds between the party-state and the non-state-sector group are weaker than those between the party-state and the state-sector group, the non-state-sector group tends to choose less conventional, more authority-challenging forms of political participation than does the state-sector group in its efforts to achieve its respective economic, social, and political objectives.

In sum, the empirical findings have confirmed my central hypotheses, as laid out in chapter 1. These hypotheses are as follows: (1) compared to the lower class, which has received less support from the party-state during the state-led, post-Mao reforms, the new Chinese middle class—especially those employed in the state apparatus—tends to be more supportive of the current party-state but less supportive of democratic values and institutions; (2) the new middle class's attitudes toward democracy may be largely accounted for by this class's close ideational and institutional ties with the state as well as its own perceived socioeconomic well-being, among other factors; and (3) the lack of support for democracy among the middle class tends to cause this social class to act in favor of the current state but in opposition to democratic change.

An important indicator of this proposition is the middle class's more active participation in elections at various levels, even though the elections are controlled by the party-state and utilized to legitimize the CCP rule.

The empirical findings from this study have provided a multifaceted picture of China's new middle class with respect to this social class's formation and its attitudinal and behavioral orientations toward democracy and toward the current CCP regime. What does this image foretell about the role of the middle class in democratization in China in particular and, by extension, in the developing world in general? I now address this important question.

III. Implications: The Middle Class as a Contingent Democratic Supporter

The empirical findings from this study have crucial political implications for the role of the middle class in democratization in China, and also may carry important theoretical implications for such a role in the developing world at large. Both implications represent an extensions of the central argument developed in this book. This central argument is that in China, as a contemporary late- or late-late-developing country, the middle class's attitudinal and behavioral orientation toward democracy and democratization is *contingent* upon salient socioeconomic and sociopolitical conditions in a society, such as the role of the state in the emergence and growth of that class and the class's ideational and institutional connection with the incumbent state.

A. Political Implications for Democratization in China

The chief political implication of this study is that China's middle class is unlikely to serve as a catalyst of democratization, either immediately or in the very near future. This is not only because most members of the class do not seem to support basic democratic norms and institutions, but also because the middle class as a whole seems to be even less democratically oriented than the lower class, which still accounts for the overwhelming majority of the population in contemporary China. Furthermore, our findings suggest that the middle class—especially the state-sector-employed subgroup, the one that currently constitutes the overwhelming majority of the middle class—would now side with the incumbent CCP government. This means that this group would turn away from political change that led to democracy, since such a change would threaten the very existence of the CCP rule. I conclude this because the new middle class is highly supportive of the fundamental norms and major public policies of the CCP government. In other words, the current party-state can still draw substantial legitimacy from the middle class, especially from those employed by the state.

Second, the findings suggest that although China's middle class is not likely to serve as the harbinger of democracy now, its current attitudes toward democracy and democratization may change in the future. A crucial shift in the middle class's orientation toward democracy could occur, if key sociopolitical conditions alter, in particular, its relationship with or dependence on the party-state and its perceived social and economic statuses. As shown throughout this book, it is mainly because China's middle class relies heavily on the authoritarian state for its survival and prosperity, and by and large is content with its current social and economic statuses, that this class is currently "undemocratic." Following the reasoning established in this study, however, the middle class may become enthusiastic about democracy and democratization if this class's dependence on the state significantly weakens and/or its perception of its social and economic statuses turns negative. Such changes in these two key variables (i.e., the middle class's ties with the party-state and its self-assessment of social and economic statuses), which have significantly influenced the middle class's orientation toward democracy, could occur in any of the following ways.

The dependence of the middle class on the state could steadily decrease as the private sector of the national economy expands. According to the findings of this study, only about 40% of the middle class in the urban areas was employed in the non-state sector as of 2007. As modernization continues to deepen and extend to more socioeconomic sectors and geographic areas across China, however, the size of the non-state-sector middle class will grow accordingly. As the private sector grows, this may not only increase the size of the middle class as a whole but also, and more importantly, pull members of the existing middle class out of the orbit of the state as more and/or better employment and career opportunities present themselves. As I have demonstrated earlier, the non-state-sector members of the middle class tend to be more supportive of democracy than are their counterparts in the state sector. Thus, as the size of that non-state-sector segment of the middle class increases, the general level of democratic support within the middle class should gradually rise.

In addition, the middle class's perception of its own social and economic statuses may well turn negative in time. This could take place as the CCP government becomes increasingly integrated with the upper classes—such as capitalists, especially "red capitalists"—at the expense of the middle class's interests. The depth and magnitude of the integration of the party-state with capitalists in China—or "the integration of power and wealth" (Dickson 2008)—has intensified drastically in the past decade. As Bruce Dickson (2008, 238) recently characterized the situation, this integration is "not an arm's length relationship," rather,

the party has integrated itself into the private sector with party branches and officially sponsored business associations, encouraged its members, including party and government officials, to "plunge into the sea" of the private sector, and recruited growing numbers of successful entrepreneurs into the party. These red capitalists represent the integration of wealth and power that is at the heart of crony communism in China.... Red capitalists own the largest firms and are more likely to participate in China's formal political institutions.

In fact, the party-state and capitalists, especially red capitalists, have consolidated and perpetuated their cozy relationship increasingly at the expense of the interests of the middle class and the lower class. Governments at various levels have increasingly made policies that favor capitalists in the name of promoting economic development, while capitalists in return have provided government officials with a good portion of the financial and other dividends they derive from these policies. Consequently, this collaboration, characterized as "crony communism" (Dickson 2008) is leading more and more middle-class members to feel squeezed. For instance, governments and real estate developers together have monopolized or manipulated housing markets for their respective financial gains, causing housing prices to skyrocket in major cities. As a result, more and more middle-class people, especially young white-collar people, find themselves unable to afford either to purchase or to rent their own homes.

Although the overall social and economic statuses of the middle class, and especially those of its state-sector group, have by no means declined to the level of the lower class, there have been some signs of such a decline in recent years. Based on a series of in-depth interviews with young and middle-aged middle-class residents in Beijing and Shanghai, Wen Mao (2010) finds that

in the past several years, the overall life style of the urban middle class has been markedly jeopardized by skyrocketing housing costs, ever-increasing everyday living expenses, overburden workload, and job insecurity. As a result, some of the middle class we interviewed felt their real living conditions had deteriorated to the level of the "lower class."

As Zhiwu Chen, a professor of economics at Yale University, suggests, the upper class in China can hedge economic risks, such as inflation, and profit from rising real estate prices with their large investments in multiple assets, including real estate. But the majority of the middle and lower class are far less well situated to endure inflation and rising housing prices, with their limited incomes and their lack of asset investments (*South Weekly* 2010, 19).

In short, as mentioned previously, the middle class's relationship with the party-state and its perceived social and economic statuses may shift in response to the changes in some fundamental socioeconomic conditions in China, such as the potential expansion of the non-state-sector segment of the middle class and the increasing "integration of power and wealth" at the expense of the interests of the middle class and the lower class. Consequently, as the middle class's dependence on the party-state lessens and as its perception of its social and economic statuses turns pessimistic, the middle class is more likely to favor democratic changes and to turn its back on the current CCP government.

It should be noted that in addition to the two key factors (i.e., dependence on the state and perception of social/economic status) closely examined in this study, other factors may also play important parts in shaping the middle class's attitudinal and behavioral orientations toward democracy and democratization. Those factors include, but are not limited to, the middle class's political alliance with or fear of other classes (e.g., upper or working classes), its own class consciousness, and its own sheer size relative to other social classes. According to earlier studies of the middle class elsewhere—especially those that employ the contingent approach (e.g., Koo 1991; Rueschemeyer et al. 1992; Brown and Jones 1995; Rodan 1993; Johnson 1985; Bell 1998; Jones

1998; Lam 1999; Torii 2003; Englehart 2003)—and recent field observations in China (e.g., *South Weekly* 2010; Mao 2010), one can conceivably speculate that the orientation of the middle class's political attitudes and behavior will be contingent upon changes in all or some of these factors.

Finally, even more critically, the findings from this study suggest that China's new middle class *as a whole* did not act democratically as of the time of the study. I have found that most middle-class respondents (over 60%) tended to participate in elections for local people's congresses, which are firmly controlled and purposefully designed by the CCP to strengthen its one-party rule. On the one hand, the findings imply that formal political institutions in China—such as the elections for local people's congresses—do not seem to provide democratic supporters within the middle class with an attractive channel for expressing their political preferences. On the other hand, these democratic supporters, while currently representing a minority of the middle class, find the less conventional yet more regime-challenging political channels—such as contacting officials and petitioning governments individually or collectively—to be more meaningful ways to register their views and demands. Consequently, one may conclude that, while the formal channels of political participation tend to solicit support for the current political system but discourage demands for democratic change from the middle class, unconventional channels facilitate a democratic tendency among the middle class.

Given these aforementioned patterns and logics of political participation pertinent to the middle class in contemporary China, it can also be argued that if the middle class becomes more democratically oriented in response to significant changes in its relationship with the party-state and its perceived social and economic conditions, this class will more frequently engage in unconventional and regime-challenging political activities, particularly petitioning the government individually and/or collectively. As this happens, more and more of the middle class will turn away from voting booths. While, as indicated

earlier, only a minority of middle-class individuals were participating in unconventional political activities as of 2007,
there appears to be a trend of increasing involvement in such
activities among the urban middle class. For example, according to recent field studies in major Chinese cities (e.g., Cai
2005; Read 2004; Tomba 2004), a substantial number of urban
middle-class residents, particularly those in the private sector, have taken unconventional actions, such as forming homeowners' associations and organizing protests to defend their
property interests and rights. Furthermore, the positive correlation I have established between participation in unconventional activities and democratic support enables me to predict
that an increase in midle-class participation in unconventional
channels may presage an emerging role of the middle class as
an agent of democratic change in China in the future.

B. Theoretical Implications in a Comparative Perspective

While the contingent approach has been strongly supported by
the empirical findings on China in this study, one may still
ask: how relevant, after all, is this theoretical framework to the
role of the middle classes in promoting democratization in other
late-developing (or late-late-developing) countries? As suggested
throughout the book, the main findings from this study are not
completely unique to the Chinese context; instead, they can be
seen in other late-developing countries. Thus, the contingent
approach should also be relevant to other developing countries.
This theoretical relevance can be further explored in the following discussion of two salient issues.

The first of these issues concerns the overarching role that
the state offen plays in the formation and growth of the middle
class in a contemporary late- or late-late-developing country.
That role can be better understood by examining two critical factors that distinguish contemporary late- or late-late-developing
countries (most of which gained national independence after

World War II) from early-industrialized countries. One factor is, as noted earlier in this book, that to meet socioeconomic challenges unique to late developers, the states in these countries must play a far more preponderant role than did the states in early-industrialized countries in the process of development. In other words, the stronger role of a late-developing country's state results from the necessity for its guidance and resources to achieve economic development and sometimes even to ensure national survival: that is, the late developer faces more severe internal and external challenges than did early industrializers, and overcoming these challenges requires a stronger state to pool a nation's resources and to design and implement strategies swiftly and effectively (see, e.g., Gerschenkron 1962; Packenham 1992; Kohli 2004).

The other factor is that the states in many contemporary, late-developing countries are arguably more powerful and sophisticated than their counterparts in the early-industrialized countries. Unlike the states in contemporary, late-developing countries, the *declining* feudal states in early-industrialized countries were usually too weak to play any decisive role in the socioeconomic transformations (Dickson 2008, 205). For these reasons, states in contemporary, late-developing countries are positioned to play a predominant role in creating and shaping the new middle classes in the process of rapid economic development.

As discussed earlier, several empirical (though non-probability-sample based) observations of contemporary, late-developing countries in East Asia, Southeast Asia, South Asia, and Latin America have asserted the critical role of the state in creating and shaping new middle classes, suggesting that the rise of the middle class in these countries has been a direct consequence of rapid state-led economic development over the past several decades. For instance, states in a number of Latin American countries, such as Brazil, Mexico, Chile, Uruguay, and Peru, played a crucial role from the 1940s through the 1980s in engineering and implementing a national economic development strategy known as import substitution industrialization (ISI). This state-sanctioned strategy, designed to survive global economic crises and to build national economies at a rapid pace in the wake of World War II, replaced foreign imports with domestic production. The process made a significant contribution to the creation of the new middle classes in both the public and the private sectors, meanwhile shaping political alliances between these classes and other social classes, as discussed in chapter 1.

Similarly, in East Asian, Southeast Asian and South Asian societies, the state also played a decisive role in economic transformation and development. While the economic development strategy eventually adopted by some of these states, export-led industrialization (ELI), differed from ISI, it also engendered the socioeconomic conditions requisite to the emergence of new middle classes in those countries. For instance, a large portion of the newly emerged middle classes in East and Southeast Asian societies is "dependent upon the state for their employment, either as public servants, or as employees of state-supported companies" (Brown and Jones 1995, 92). In India, "the state-managed model of economic planning and development" (Fernandes 2006, 20) created the new middle class in post-independent India, mainly through state educational policies and state employment. According to Fernandes (2006, 20), therefore, the middle class in India has been "shaped by a continued strong dependence on the state."

In sum, the direct result of these active state interventions in the economy, which went on to induce the formation of the middle classes in East/Southeast/South Asian and Latin American societies, is that these classes became highly dependent upon state patronage (Rueschemeyer et al. 1992; Brown and Jones 1995; Bell 1998; Jones 1998; Torii 2003; Fernandes 2006). Thus, just as in the story told in this study, the explanation of the role of the middle class in fostering democracy must be a contingent one.

The second issue, related to the comparative theoretical implications of the findings from this study, concerns variations within the middle class, especially along the line of the middle class's relationship with the state. As the contingent approach suggests, to achieve development goals, the state in some late- or late-late-developing countries often makes relentless efforts to expand and guide *both* public and private sectors of national economies. This has been the case in China and other late-developing countries in East Asia, Southeast Asia, South Asia, and Latin America, as mentioned above.

As a result, the middle class in these countries is typically divided into two major groups, state-sector and non-state-sector groups. On the one hand, both groups are created and shaped by the strong state in the late-developing country; as demonstrated in this book, the middle class as a whole is to be distinguished from other classes, especially the lower class. On the other hand, each of the two subgroups in the middle class is likely to differ from each other in its political views and behavior, due to its respective relationship with the state. As Ulf Sundhaussen (1991, 112–113) contends, therefore, inquiry into the political orientation of the middle class in the developing world "would have to begin with distinguishing between the different kinds of Middle Classes." Furthermore, he observes that "the salaried professionals, often in state employment, are usually too dependent on their employer, especially if the state has been organized along patrimonial lines.... Only, the intellectuals, academics, lawyers and journalists can reasonably be expected in Third World countries to champion the cause of democracy" (Sundhaussen 1991, 113).

Some non-survey-based empirical studies of late-developing countries in East Asia, Southeast Asia, South Asia, and Latin America have found similar differences within the new middle classes. For instance, in Malaysia, Singapore, the Philippines, Thailand, and South Korea, a large portion of the middle class was once employed in the state bureaucracy, and enjoyed strong connections with the government authorities. This portion of the middle class generally supported the consolidation of authoritarian rule (Brown and Jones 1995; Bell 1998; Jones 1998; Englehart 2003; Shin 1999), because it was the main beneficiary of the state policies and had a vested interest in the continuity and stability of authoritarian rule (Bell 1998). Yet, in these countries, a portion of the middle classes in the non-state sector, which consists of professionals and managers, tended to be more progressive and was more likely to demand democracy than the state-sector portion, even though it was much less assertive than the lower class. In today's India, the segment of the middle class that was employed in the state apparatus has enjoyed "specific economic benefits in terms of employment, as well as with specific forms of political capital" (Fernandes 2006, 23). Given its strong connection with and dependence on the state, this segment of the middle class tends to be supportive of government policies. But the segment of the middle class connected to the non-state apparatus seems to be "dissatisfied and [to have] pressed the state" (Fernandes 2006, 25) for economic benefits—such as job security and job opportunities—and for political power. These non-state-apparatus segments of the middle class tend to have views on government policies that differ from those of the state-apparatus segment of the middle class, although they can also be distinguished from the lower and upper classes.

All told, this discussion of political and theoretical implications of the study's empirical findings amounts to an extension of the central argument that has been advanced in this book: the attitudinal and behavioral orientations of the middle class— as a whole and in part—toward democratic change in late- or late-late-developing countries are contingent upon its relationship with the incumbent state, along with its perceived social and economic well-being. The bottom line is that the middle class's support for democracy and democratization in these countries is far from inevitable.

To conclude, understanding the role of the middle class in democratization in late- or late-late-developing countries is not self-evident. But, as the size and influence of this class constantly increases in most of these countries, any serious exploration of the prospects for democratic change must entail a firm grasp of that class's role in these changes.

Appendix

List of In-Depth Interviews Conducted in Beijing, Chengdu, and Xi'an in 2008

A set of in-depth interviews was conducted with 223 residents in the same cities as those where the probability-sample survey was conducted—Beijing, Chengdu, and Xi'an—in March and April 2008. The interviewees were purposefully selected to represent various segments of the urban population, including middle-class individuals employed in both the state sector and non-state sector. To explore more nuanced explanations of the results from the probability-sample survey, the research team asked the interviewees to deliberate on several key issues that were also tackled in the probability-sample survey. On average, each interview lasted about two hours. The serial number and date of each interview, as well as the age, residence, and occupation of each interviewee, are listed in the following table.

No.	Date	Age	City	Occupation
1	3/1/2008	28	Beijing	Small Businessperson
2	4/28/2008	65	Beijing	Professor
3	3/31/2008	34	Chengdu	Journalist
4	4/28/2008	33	Chengdu	Assistant Professor
5	4/2/2008	32	Xi'an	Salesman
6	3/29/2008	31	Xi'an	Elementary School Teacher
7	4/8/2008	44	Beijing	Professor
8	4/29/2008	35	Xi'an	Chief Editor
9	3/8/2008	42	Beijing	Professor
10	3/2/2008	29	Beijing	Finance Manager
11	3/28/2008	45	Beijing	Executive Director in Non-governmental Organization
12	3/29/2008	50	Beijing	State-Owned-Enterprise Manager
13	4/1/2008	42	Beijing	Lawyer
14	4/7/2008	53	Beijing	Collective-Owned-Enterprise Manager
15	3/29/2008	40	Xi'an	Government Official
16	3/29/2008	45	Xi'an	Middle School Teacher
17	3/29/2008	37	Xi'an	Government Official
18	4/8/2008	53	Beijing	Professor
19	4/2/2008	40	Chengdu	Small Businessperson
20	4/4/2008	30	Chengdu	Senior Manager
21	4/4/2008	39	Chengdu	Assistant Professor
22	4/4/2008	39	Chengdu	Professor
23	4/2/2008	42	Chengdu	Small Businessperson
24	4/4/2008	35	Chengdu	Journalist
25	4/4/2008	47	Chengdu	Professor
26	4/2/2008	45	Chengdu	Small Share Speculator
27	4/1/2008	38	Chengdu	Associate Professor
28	4/29/2008	50	Chengdu	Engineer in State-Owned Enterprise
29	4/2/2008	28	Chengdu	Sales Manager
30	4/12/2008	24	Chengdu	Accountant in Foreign Company
31	4/8/2008	38	Beijing	Party Cadre in District Propaganda Department
32	4/11/2008	48	Xi'an	Government Official
33	4/10/2008	25	Xi'an	Assistant Manager
34	4/11/2008	46	Xi'an	Government Official
35	4/12/2008	48	Xi'an	Government Official
36	4/11/2008	24	Xi'an	Assistant to the Owner of a Private Corporation
37	4/12/2008	27	Xi'an	Small Shareholder
38	4/12/2008	43	Xi'an	Independent Scholar

No.	Date	Age	City	Occupation
39	4/12/2008	45	Xi'an	Doctor in Public Hospital
40	4/12/2008	54	Xi'an	Taxi Driver
41	4/12/2008	33	Xi'an	Manager in Joint Venture
42	4/13/2008	32	Xi'an	Lawyer
43	4/13/2008	36	Xi'an	Owner of Several Apartments
44	4/13/2008	35	Xi'an	Researcher in Public Organization
45	4/13/2008	35	Xi'an	Elementary School Teacher
46	4/13/2008	60	Xi'an	Singer
47	4/13/2008	58	Xi'an	Artist
48	4/21/2008	56	Xi'an	Self-Employed Worker
49	4/21/2008	33	Xi'an	Tour Guide
50	4/21/2008	45	Xi'an	University Staff
51	4/21/2008	42	Xi'an	University Staff
52	3/17/2008	34	Beijing	Street Office Staff
53	3/18/2008	37	Beijing	Professor
54	3/18/2008	41	Beijing	Accountant in Foreign Company
55	3/18/2008	24	Beijing	Lawyer in Foreign Company
56	3/18/2008	27	Beijing	Assistant Manager in Foreign Company
57	3/18/2008	32	Beijing	Independent Scholar
58	3/18/2008	31	Beijing	Freelance Writer
59	3/19/2008	39	Beijing	Magazine Editor
60	3/19/2008	45	Beijing	Architect Designer in Private Enterprise
61	3/19/2008	46	Beijing	Person Living on Bank Interests
62	3/19/2008	47	Beijing	Small Shareholder in Private Enterprise
63	3/19/2008	57	Beijing	Manager in State-Owned Enterprise
64	3/19/2008	56	Beijing	Beijing Municipal Official
65	3/19/2008	55	Beijing	Scientific Researcher in Public Organization
66	3/19/2008	52	Beijing	Professor
67	3/19/2008	34	Beijing	Independent Translator
68	3/19/2008	45	Beijing	Educational Broker
69	3/18/2008	45	Beijing	Real Estate Broker
70	3/17/2008	51	Beijing	District Office Staff
71	3/17/2008	27	Beijing	Website Designer
72	3/19/2008	28	Beijing	Website Editor
73	3/19/2008	29	Beijing	Media Broker
74	3/19/2008	30	Beijing	Freelance Writer
75	3/6/2008	43	Chengdu	Owner of a Teahouse

No.	Date	Age	City	Occupation
76	3/6/2008	45	Chengdu	Small Businessperson
77	3/6/2008	34	Chengdu	Small Shareholder in Stock Market
78	3/6/2008	37	Chengdu	Owner of Several Apartments
79	3/6/2008	38	Chengdu	Independent Scholar
80	3/6/2008	29	Chengdu	Freelance Writer
81	3/6/2008	25	Chengdu	Independent Translator
82	3/6/2008	27	Chengdu	Salesperson
83	3/8/2008	29	Chengdu	Assistant Manager in Joint Venture
84	3/8/2008	41	Chengdu	Municipal Government Official
85	3/8/2008	43	Chengdu	Municipal Government Official
86	3/9/2008	34	Chengdu	Photographer
87	3/9/2008	32	Chengdu	Program Developer in Technology Company
88	3/9/2008	47	Chengdu	District Office Staff
89	3/9/2008	56	Chengdu	Owner of a Small Restaurant
90	3/9/2008	54	Chengdu	Staff in Public Organization
91	3/9/2008	53	Chengdu	Doctor in Public Hospital
92	3/9/2008	58	Chengdu	Owner of Several Apartments
93	3/9/2008	60	Chengdu	Professor
94	3/25/2008	45	Xi'an	Municipal Government Official
95	3/25/2008	42	Xi'an	District Office Staff
96	3/25/2008	43	Xi'an	District Office Staff
97	3/25/2008	38	Xi'an	Manager in Foreign Company
98	3/25/2008	37	Xi'an	Manager in Foreign Company
99	3/26/2008	39	Xi'an	Journalist
100	3/26/2008	37	Xi'an	Independent Artist
101	3/26/2008	46	Xi'an	Singer
102	3/26/2008	47	Xi'an	Dancer
103	3/26/2008	52	Xi'an	Professional Sports Coach
104	3/26/2008	53	Xi'an	Freelance Writer
105	3/26/2008	53	Xi'an	Self-Employed Worker
106	3/26/2008	54	Xi'an	Small Shareholder in Private Enterprise
107	3/27/2008	29	Xi'an	Professional Soccer Player
108	3/27/2008	28	Xi'an	Professional Soccer Player
109	3/27/2008	32	Xi'an	Tour Guide
110	3/27/2008	34	Xi'an	Tour Guide
111	3/27/2008	35	Xi'an	Technologist in State-Owned Enterprise
112	3/27/2008	35	Xi'an	Data Analyst in State-Owned Enterprise

No.	Date	Age	City	Occupation
113	3/11/2008	24	Beijing	Professional Athlete
114	3/11/2008	25	Beijing	Professional Athlete
115	3/11/2008	25	Beijing	Professional Athlete
116	3/11/2008	26	Beijing	Professional Dancer
117	3/11/2008	27	Beijing	Singer
118	3/11/2008	45	Beijing	Independent Film Maker
119	3/12/2008	46	Beijing	Exhibition Designer
120	3/12/2008	46	Beijing	TV Program Editor
121	3/12/2008	60	Beijing	Professor
122	3/12/2008	58	Beijing	Artist
123	3/12/2008	57	Beijing	Freelance Writer
124	3/12/2008	56	Beijing	Bank Manager
125	3/13/2008	54	Beijing	Opera Performer
126	3/13/2008	30	Beijing	Financial Analyst
127	3/13/2008	32	Beijing	Independent Economist
128	3/13/2008	33	Beijing	Financial Broker
129	3/13/2008	34	Beijing	Self-Employed Worker
130	4/22/2008	41	Chengdu	Independent Columnist
131	4/22/2008	47	Chengdu	Owner of Tour Company
132	4/22/2008	48	Chengdu	Middle School Teacher
133	4/22/2008	48	Chengdu	Lawyer/Owner of a Small Law Firm
134	4/22/2008	51	Chengdu	Accountant in State-Owned Enterprise
135	4/23/2008	50	Chengdu	Car Broker
136	4/23/2008	30	Chengdu	Real Estate Broker
137	4/23/2008	36	Chengdu	Data Analyst in Foreign Company
138	4/23/2008	37	Chengdu	Consultant in Joint Venture
139	4/23/2008	35	Chengdu	Independent Investment Consultant
140	4/23/2008	41	Chengdu	Arts Broker
141	4/24/2008	29	Chengdu	Stock Market Speculator
142	4/24/2008	28	Chengdu	Manager in State-Owned Bank
143	4/24/2008	27	Chengdu	Singer
144	4/24/2008	41	Chengdu	Manager in State-Owned Enterprise
145	4/24/2008	42	Chengdu	Doctor in Public Hospital
146	3/7/2008	52	Xi'an	Street Office Staff
147	3/7/2008	51	Xi'an	Street Office Staff
148	3/7/2008	54	Xi'an	Municipal Government Official
149	3/7/2008	42	Xi'an	Financial Analyst in Private Firm
150	3/7/2008	34	Xi'an	Self-Employed Worker
151	3/15/2008	32	Xi'an	Owner of Upscale Restaurant

No.	Date	Age	City	Occupation
152	3/15/2008	37	Xi'an	Small Shareholder in High-Tech Company
153	3/15/2008	38	Xi'an	Law Consultant for Foreign Company
154	3/15/2008	35	Xi'an	Marketing Manager for Joint Venture
155	3/15/2008	45	Xi'an	Public Relations Manager in State-Owned Enterprise
156	4/19/2008	44	Xi'an	District Government Official
157	4/19/2008	45	Xi'an	Municipal Government Official
158	4/19/2008	43	Xi'an	Vice Director in Public Organization
159	4/19/2008	47	Xi'an	Researcher in High-Tech Company
160	4/29/2008	48	Xi'an	Small Businessperson
161	4/29/2008	49	Xi'an	Sales Director in Collective-Owned Enterprise
162	4/29/2008	50	Xi'an	Party Cadre in Municipal Propaganda Department
163	4/29/2008	52	Xi'an	Doctor in Private Hospital
164	4/29/2008	55	Xi'an	Professor in Private University
165	3/31/2008	25	Xi'an	Arts Performer
166	3/31/2008	24	Xi'an	Arts Collector
167	3/31/2008	29	Xi'an	Department Director in City of Xi'an
168	3/31/2008	28	Xi'an	Technologist in State-Owned Telecommunication Company
169	3/31/2008	30	Xi'an	Manager in Private Enterprise
170	3/30/2009	31	Xi'an	Independent Columnist
171	3/30/2009	32	Xi'an	Freelance Writer
172	3/30/2009	33	Xi'an	Sales Director in Private Enterprise
173	3/30/2009	38	Xi'an	Data Analyst in Public Organization
174	4/18/2008	34	Beijing	District Judge
175	4/18/2008	56	Beijing	Lawyer
176	4/18/2008	54	Beijing	Middle School Teacher
177	4/18/2008	44	Beijing	Doctor in Public Hospital
178	4/18/2008	43	Beijing	Pharmacist
179	4/7/2008	23	Beijing	Pianist
180	4/7/2008	34	Beijing	Film Actor
181	4/7/2008	53	Beijing	Arts Collector
182	4/7/2008	45	Beijing	Stock Market Speculator

No.	Date	Age	City	Occupation
183	4/6/2008	46	Beijing	Manager in Collective-Owned Enterprise
184	4/6/2008	57	Beijing	District Government Official
185	4/6/2008	58	Beijing	Municipal Party Cadre in Organization Department
186	4/6/2008	43	Beijing	Statistician in Private Enterprise
187	4/6/2008	47	Beijing	Staff in Public Organization
188	4/5/2008	48	Beijing	Researcher in Public Hospital
189	4/5/2008	49	Beijing	Data Analyst in Finance Company
190	4/5/2008	50	Beijing	Professor
191	4/5/2008	31	Beijing	Freelance Writer
192	4/5/2008	33	Beijing	Movie Star
193	3/23/2008	32	Chengdu	Independent Film Maker
194	3/23/2008	34	Chengdu	Tour Guide
195	3/23/2008	45	Chengdu	Manager in Private Enterprise
196	3/23/2008	46	Chengdu	Founder of a Law Firm
197	3/14/2008	60	Chengdu	Independent Scholar
198	3/14/2008	54	Chengdu	Lawyer in State-Owned Enterprise
199	3/14/2008	32	Chengdu	Vice Director in Non-governmental Organization
200	3/14/2008	45	Chengdu	Government Official
201	3/14/2008	28	Chengdu	Street Office Staff
202	4/17/2008	29	Chengdu	Journalist
203	4/17/2008	39	Chengdu	Editor in a Publishing Company
204	4/17/2008	38	Chengdu	Fashion Designer
205	4/17/2008	41	Chengdu	Photographer
206	4/17/2008	42	Chengdu	Consultant in Private Enterprise
207	4/27/2008	54	Chengdu	Researcher in Public Organization
208	4/27/2008	56	Chengdu	Manager in State-Owned Enterprise
209	4/27/2008	29	Chengdu	Dancer
210	4/27/2008	45	Chengdu	Party Cadre in District Organization Department
211	4/27/2008	46	Chengdu	Self-Employed Worker
212	4/27/2008	43	Chengdu	Small Businessperson
213	4/3/2008	42	Xi'an	Small Shareholder in Real Estate Company
214	4/8/2008	40	Xi'an	Public Relations Broker
215	3/5/3008	35	Xi'an	Technician in High-Tech Company

No.	Date	Age	City	Occupation
216	3/5/3008	34	Xi'an	Researcher in Foreign Company
217	3/5/3008	36	Xi'an	Cultural Performer in Private Cultural Company
218	3/5/3008	56	Xi'an	Stock Market Speculator
219	4/26/2008	57	Xi'an	Owner of a Tour Company
220	4/26/2008	30	Xi'an	Professional Athlete
221	4/26/2008	31	Xi'an	Independent Translator
222	3/16/2008	34	Xi'an	Editor at Publishing Company
223	3/16/2008	42	Xi'an	Vice Director in Public Research Center

Notes

Chapter 1

1. In this book, I distinguish the middle class from "private entrepreneurs" (or "capitalists" and "bourgeoisie")—particularly those who own large and medium-sized of firms—in China. The definition and identification of the middle class in this study is based on the theoretical framework of class studies mainly in sociology (e.g., Erikson and Goldthorpe 1992; Glassman 1995, 1997; Wright 1997). For the most recent studies of Chinese private entrepreneurs (as opposed to the middle class defined in this book), see, for example, the works by Dickson (2003, 2008), Tsai (2002, 2007), and Chen and Dickson (2008, 2010), which are at least in part inspired or intrigued by Barrington Moore's oft-cited argument, "no bourgeois, no democracy" (Moore 1966, 418). The reasons to distinguish the middle class from capitalists/bourgeoisie in this study will be discussed in detail in chapter 2.
2. For example, Kevin O'Brien and Rachel Stern (2008) recently advocated the need for more systematic and intensive studies of the middle class's political attitudes and behavior in China.
3. The term *unilinear* was drawn from the study of the middle classes in Asia by Hattori and Funatsu (2003).
4. While the "bourgeois" class in Moore's work differs from the middle class in this study, Moore's argument on the role of the bourgeois class has repeatedly been quoted in other studies of the middle classes.
5. As exceptions, there were only a very few studies of the middle classes in the developing world that fully or partially support this approach (see, e.g., Glassman 1991; Hsiao and Koo 1997; So and Kwitko 1990).
6. There are some registered parties other than the CCP. All these parties are firmly controlled by the CCP, and therefore are considered the satellite parties of the CCP.

7. For examples of criticisms, see the works by Mitchell (1991) and Migdal (2001).
8. Some of the most recent examples of application include the insightful studies of the role of the state in socioeconomic development in developing countries by Wade (1990), Woo-Comings (1999), Oi (1999), Pempel (1999), Bellin (2000), Kohli (2004), Chibber (2003), and Zhou (2004).
9. For the core of modernization theory, see the work by Rostow (1991). For comprehensive reviews of the modernization literature, see the works by Huntington (1971) and by Przeworski and Limongi (1997).
10. According to Packenham (1992, 16–17), this peculiar international economic condition includes "the terms of trade" that tend to move systematically against late developers and the keener international competition than that faced by earlier industrializers.
11. Nonetheless, almost none of these studies are based on representative samples of middle-class individuals, samples that could provide more robust and conclusive findings on the attitudes of the middle class toward democratization. Nor has there been such representative-sample studies of the political orientation of the middle class in a *Communist Party–ruled*, late-developing society, such as China.
12. The elections for the new people's deputies in the three survey sites— Beijing, Chengdu, and Xi'an—were conducted between September and December 2006 (see http://news.xinhuanet.com/politics/2006-11/08/content_5306507.htm).
13. According to our agreement with the officials of the streets selected in the sample, the names of these streets must remain confidential.
14. For detailed discussion on the distinction between these two kinds of survey results, see, for example, the study by Manion (1994).
15. For more detailed discussion on the generalizability of findings about relationships between variables from single- and multiple-location samples in the study of contemporary China, see, for example, works by Manion (1994) and Walder (1989).
16. For example, based on a survey carried out in four rural counties, Manion (1996) and Jennings (1997, 1998) identified the patterns of electoral connections and the correlates of political participation in rural China. Drawing on surveys in several cities, Tang (2005) has convincingly established the correlations between urban residents' views of various sociopolitical issues and different sociodemographic factors.

CHAPTER 2

1. As a neo-Marxist analyst, Erik Olin Wright (1997) used three subdimensions—means of production, position in authority structure, and possession of skills and expertise—to operationalize social class.
2. In the Chinese bureaucratic system there are four bureaucratic ranks: *bu* (ministry), *ju* (bureau), *chu* (division), and *ke* (section). Specifically,

administrative personnel of state affairs and social affairs include those bureaucrats having bureaucratic ranks higher than *chu* in the central government or provincial governments and those having bureaucratic ranks higher than *ke* in the local governments.

3. Most workers are not well educated and have a lower economic status than other social segments such as administrative personnel of state affairs and social affairs, managerial personnel, private entrepreneurs, professionals, civil servants, and self-employed individuals, and they are becoming increasingly proletariatized. See Whyte (1999), Weston (2000), and Lee (2000).

4. Since the 1950s, the Chinese party-state designed a household registration (*hukou*) system to divide China into two parts: rural and urban. The household registration (*hukou*) system was established by the Chinese party-state in 1955 as "one of its procedures for solidifying administrative control" and it distinguished rural from urban and restricted the migration from rural to urban. Moreover, urban residents enjoyed certain privileges such as access to education, housing, health care, all but the most menial jobs, and so on. There was little chance for a rural peasant to become an urban resident. See Wu and Treiman (2004).

5. For the use of this occupation-based, qualitative measure in identifying the middle class, in the Western settings, see Erikson and Goldthorpe (1992), Glassman (1995), and Wright (1997); in the Pacific Asian settings, see Hattori, Funatsu, and Torii (2003) and Hsiao and So (1999); in the Chinese settings, see Xueyi Lu and his associates (2002, 2004) and Zhang (2005).

6. Our figure of the middle class is much higher than Xueyi Lu and his associates' result (11%). There is one important reason for such a difference: our result is based on three major cities (Beijing, Cheng'du, and Xi'an), which tend to have more middle-class individuals than rural areas. Xueyi Lu and his associates' result is based on the national survey, which includes both rural and urban areas.

7. According Victor Nee (1989), "the *market power* thesis argues that as markets replace redistributive mechanisms in the allocation and distribution of goods, there is a shift in the sources of power from the redistributive sector [i.e., state sector] to the marketplace."

8. The middle class here is defined according to the qualitative branch of the objective approach (discussed earlier in this chapter), which mainly includes managerial personnel, professionals, and white-collar office workers in urban China.

9. Based on the estimate offered by Xueyi Lu and his associates (2004), I calculated the percentage of middle class in Chinese society in 1949. If I group managers, office workers, and professionals together, the middle class constituted approximately only 3% of the Chinese population.

10. I calculated the percentage of middle class in Chinese society in 1949. If I group managers, civil servants, professionals, and self-employed

laborers together, the middle class constituted approximately 7% of the Chinese population. This small but gradually rising middle class had gained some economic and/or political independence under the rule of the Nationalist Party and had a greater degree of self-determination in regard to such matters as their life style and occupational advancement, much like their counterparts in Western societies.

11. The Chinese constitution has been changed four times due to the changes in national politics. The 1954 Constitution of the People's Republic of China was promulgated by the National People's Congress on September 20, 1954. The 1954 Constitution was replaced in the midst of the Cultural Revolution by the 1975 Constitution of the People's Republic of China to reflect the politics of the Cultural Revolution. This constitution was superseded in 1978 by the 1978 Constitution of the People's Republic of China. Both the 1975 Constitution and the 1978 Constitution display the effects of the Cultural Revolution. The current constitution is the 1982 Constitution of the People's Republic of China, which was adopted by the National People's Congress on December 4, 1982. The 1982 Constitution reflects Deng Xiaoping's determination to lay a lasting institutional foundation for China's modernization, and it downplays the importance of class struggle and places top priority on development.

12. According to the official definition, the work unit is "an independent accounting unit with three characteristics: (1) administratively, it is an independent organization; (2) fiscally, it has an independent budget and produces its own accounting tables of earnings and deficits; (3) financially, it has independent accounts in banks and has legal rights to sign contracts with government or business entities" (Wu 2002, 1073).

13. The individual businesses are only permitted to employ less than eight non-family employees.

14. The private enterprises are those who employ more than eight non-family employees.

15. According to the "Tentative Stipulations," private enterprises are profitable economic organizations that are owned by individuals and employ more than eight people (International Finance Corporation 2000).

16. In the Chinese bureaucratic system there are four bureaucratic ranks: *bu* (ministry), *ju* (bureau), *chu* (division), and *ke* (section). Specifically, administrative personnel of state affairs and social affairs include those bureaucrats having bureaucratic ranks higher than *chu* in the central government or provincial governments and those having bureaucratic ranks higher than *ke* in the local governments.

17. The private enterprises are those which employ more than eight non-family employees.

18. This term is borrowed from Victor Nee (1991). The meaning of "closed" here is that the access to such positions is subject to party screening. Such positions are not open for all people to compete.

19. While classical corporatism (see Schmitter 1974) emphasizes the role of corporate institutions and organizations formed between the government and societal groups in influencing government decision making, "state corporatism" used in the context of the study of authoritarian states usually refers instead to a process by which the state uses officially recognized organizations as a tool for restricting public participation in the political process and limiting the power of civil society. For detailed discussion on state corporatism in China, see, for example, the works by Unger and Chan (1995) and Oi (1999).

20. Our three-city survey contains a question that is designed to assess the middle class's level of participation in a variety of corporatist organizations. The question is as follows: "Now I am going to read off a list of corporatist organizations; for each one, could you tell me whether you are a member or not a member of that type of organization? 1) government-sponsored trade unions, 2) state-initiated religious or church organizations, 3) state-initiated trade associations (*hangye xiehui*), 4) state-initiated citizen rights-resistance associations, 5) state-initiated social welfare groups, 6) government-sponsored professional associations, 7) government-sponsored academic organizations, 8) federation of women unions, and 9) government-sponsored sports and recreation organizations."

CHAPTER 3

1. In a probability sample, each member of a certain population should have an equal chance of selection determined by the sampling procedure. For a more detailed definition of probability sample, see, for example, the work by Floyd Fowler (1988).

2. In this study, I pooled the rest of our sample together (excluding the private entrepreneurs of mid- and large-size firms and ranking government officials who account for only about 2.5% of our sample) to form a non-middle-class category. This category accounted for 73% of our sample, which included blue-collar industrial workers (skilled and non-skilled) in state-owned, collectively owned, and privately owned enterprises; blue-collar employees in all types of service sectors; the self-employed (e.g., *getihu*) with very little capital; the unemployed, underemployed, and retirees; and college students. This category is compared with the middle-class respondents in terms of their democratic support.

3. A similar question was also asked in the East Asian Barometer (EAB) survey conducted in China. The result of the question from that survey is identical with the result from our survey. For the EAB survey, see, for example, Nathan (2007).

4. The eigenvalue of the first extracted factor is 2.66. The eigenvalue of the second factor is 0.95. $N = 739$.

5. For example, Gibson et al. (1992, 352) had the similar finding from their study of the former Soviet Union: "nearly all of the Moscow

respondents claimed a great number of rights, especially the rights most closely connected to democratic participation." As a result, they found that right consciousness has a weak loading on the factor of democratic values.

6. This finding has been substantiated by the results from the bivariate analyses (*compare means*) shown in Table 3.5.

7. Interview with the director of inspection department in the bureau of finance in the city of Xi'an, March 25, 2008.

8. Their operationalized measure of regime legitimacy or diffuse support has been used in several cross-nation and single-nation studies of political support (see, e.g., Muller 1977; Muller and Williams 1980; Finkel, Muller, Jukam, and Seligson 1989; Seligson and Muller 1987; Muller, Seligson and Fu 1989).

9. The mean of the interitem correlations of this set of items is .45; the reliability coefficient among these items is .83.

CHAPTER 4

1. According to Gerschenkron (1962), the "late developers" (or late-developing countries) are those countries that joined the global tide of development when it was already in rapid motion. As a result, the developing countries, such as China, and newly industrialized countries can be considered later developers, since they commenced their processes of economic development when economic development was already in rapid motion or had reached maturity in Western Europe and North America.

2. For a detailed discussion on the role of the state in creating/shaping private entrepreneurs (or capitalists) as well as the latter's attitudes toward democracy in China, see, for example, the studies by Pearson (1997), Dickson (2003), Tsai (2005, 2006), and Chen and Dickson (2010).

3. It is also important to examine the impact of the distinction between employment in government/party administrative agencies and that in state-owned business/industrial enterprises on democratic support among those who were employed within the state apparatus in general. Regrettably, our survey did not include specific (or at least direct) questions to identify this distinction.

4. Interview with the owner of a law firm in the city of Chengdu, April 22, 2008.

5. A factor analysis was conducted of these two items in the responses of both classes. From the factor analysis, only one dominant factor emerged, which explained 65% of the original variance. The factor scores will be used as the collective indicator of satisfaction with social and economic statuses in the multivariate analysis that follows.

6. Interview with the middle-level manager in the state-owned enterprise in the city of Beijing, March 19, 2008.

7. Interview with the financial analyst in one foreign company in the city of Beijing, March 13, 2008.

8. A multiple regression model (OLS) is often used to analyze cross-section survey data of this sort. Nonetheless, an OLS model may suffer from underestimation of coefficient variances and standard errors, due to a high degree of heteroscedasticity of data. To address this concern, therefore, we conducted White's test to detect heteroscedasticity. The results from the test indicated that there was not a serious heteroscedasticity in our data set. As a result, OLS can be considered suitable for the analysis of our data.

9. The coefficient of the interaction term between diffuse support and membership in the middle class is negative and statistically significant. The total effect of diffuse support within the middle class, measured by the unstandardized coefficient, is -1.1. It was the sum of -0.923 for diffuse support *without* the interaction term of the middle class and -0.177 for diffuse support *with* the interaction term of the middle class.

10. The coefficient of the interaction term between employment in the state apparatus and membership in the middle class is negative and statistically significant. The total effect of employment in the state apparatus on democratic support within the middle class, measured by the unstandardized coefficient, is -1.752. It was the sum of -1.232 for employment in the state apparatus *without* the interaction term of the middle class and -0.520 for employment in the state apparatus *with* the interaction term of the middle class.

11. The coefficient of the interaction term between satisfaction with social and economic status and membership in the middle class is negative and statistically significant. The total effect of satisfaction with social and economic status within the middle class, measured by the unstandardized coefficient, is -1.23. It was the sum of -0.452 for satisfaction *without* the interaction term of the middle class and -0.778 for satisfaction *with* the interaction term of the middle class.

CHAPTER 5

1. The exploratory factor analysis here is the statistical technique used to identify the underlying structure of the collection of all seven participation items.

2. Article 97 of the 1982 Constitution of the People's Republic China provides that "deputies to the people's congresses of counties, cities not divided into districts, municipal districts, townships, nationality townships and towns are elected directly by their constituencies" (see National People's Congress 1982.).

3. In this procedure, the initial lists of nominees generated from electorate deliberations are submitted to the local election committees, considered, and returned back to the electors, who further deliberate, passing the list back up to the election committees and so forth for "three ups and three downs" (McCormick 1996, 40).

4. The "four cardinal principles" include (1) supporting the CCP's leadership, (2) adhering to socialism, (3) upholding

Marxism-Leninism-Mao Zedong thought, and (4) maintaining the proletarian dictatorship (see Wang 1999, 57).

5. For example, in 1980 at Beijing University and Hunan Normal University, some candidates advocated some radical ideas in "publicized" electoral campaigns in local people's congress elections (see Nathan 1985, 193–223; McCormick 1996, 40–41).

6. See Chapter One: General Principles of the 1982 Constitution of the People's Republic (National People's Congress 1982).

7. The "spiritual gains" here refer to the individual's satisfaction from expression of values through voting or non-voting.

8. It was until July 2005 that the Chinese National People's Congress issued the "Law of Property Rights in the People's Republic of China." According to the "Law of Property Rights," homeowners may establish homeowners' associations in their neighborhoods, and it does endow ordinary homeowners with the right to organize homeowners' associations. However, in practice, local governments put many limits on the organization of homeowners' associations by ordinary homeowners. As a result, homeowners' associations almost did not exist in many neighborhoods, and for those that existed, their autonomy was severely impacted by the local government.

9. Since the purpose of this part of the chapter is to study the impacts of the middle class's democratic values on its own political behavior, this regression model is executed within the middle-class category.

CHAPTER 6

1. For a summary of this line of thinking, see, for example, the work by Hattori, Funatsu, and Torii (2003).

REFERENCES

Acemoglu, Daron, and James A. Robinson. 2000. "Why Did the West Extend the Franchise? Democracy, Inequality and Growth in Historical Perspective." *Quarterly Journal of Economics* 115 (4): 1167–1199.

Alford, Robert R. 1962. "A Suggested Index of the Association of Social Class and Voting." *Public Opinion Quarterly* 26: 417–425.

Almond, Gabriel, and Sidney Verba. 1963. *The Civic Culture: Political Attitudes and Democracy in Five Nations.* Princeton, NJ: Princeton University Press.

Amsden, Alice H. 1985. "The State and Taiwan's Economic Development." In *Bringing the State Back In,* ed. Peter Evans, Dietrich Rueschemeyer, and Theda Skocpol, 78–106. New York: Cambridge University Press.

Amsden, Alice H. 1989. *Asia's Next Giant: South Korea and Late Industrialization.* New York: Oxford University Press.

Archive Research Office of the Central Committee of the Chinese Communist Party. 1994. *Deng xiaoping jianshe you zhongguo tesi de shehuizhuyi lunshu zhuanti zhaibian* (Special Digest of Deng Xiaoping's Works on Building Socialism with the Chinese Characteristics). Beijing: Central Archive Press.

Bahry, Donna, and Brian D. Silver. 1990. "Soviet Citizen Participation on the Eve of Democratization." *American Political Science Review* 48 (September): 820–847.

Baum, Richard. 1994. *Burying Mao: Chinese Politics in the Age of Deng Xiaoping.* Princeton, NJ: Princeton University Press.

Baviskar, Amita, and Raka Ray, ed. 2011. *Elite and Everyman: The Cultural Politics of the Indian Middle Classes.* New York: Routledge.

Bell, Daniel A. 1998. "After the Tsunami: Will Economic Crisis Bring Democracy to Asia." *New Republic* 218 (10) (March 9, 1998): 22–25.

Bellin, Eva. 2000. "Contingent Democrats: Industrialists, Labor, and Democratization in Late-Developing Countries." *World Politics* 52 (2): 175–205.

Bellin, Eva. 2002. *Stalled Democracy: Capital, Labor and the Paradox of State-Sponsored Development*. Ithaca, NY: Cornell University Press.

Bertrand, Jachues. 1998. "Growth and Democracy in Southeast Asia." *Comparative Politics* 30 (3): 355–375.

Bian, Yanjie. 2002. "Chinese Social Stratification and Social Mobility." *Annual Review of Sociology* 28: 91–116.

Bian, Yanjie, and John R. Logan. 1996. "Market Transition and the Persistence of Power: The Changing Stratification System in Urban China." *American Sociological Review* 61 (5): 739–758.

Brown, David, and David Martin Jones. 1995. "Democratization and the Myth of the Liberalizing Middle Classes." In *Towards Illiberal Democracy in Pacific Asia*, ed. Daniel A. Bell et al., 78–106. Basingstoke, Hampshire: Macmillan.

Bunce, Valerie, Michael McFaul, and Kathryn Stoner-Weiss. 2010. "Waves and Troughs of Democracy and Dictatorship." In *Democracy and Authoritarianism in the Postcommunist World*, ed. Valerie Bunce, Michael McFaul, and Kathryn Stoner-Weiss, vii–xi. New York: Cambridge University Press.

Burns, John P. 1999. "The People's Republic of China at 50: National Political Reform." *The China Quarterly* 159 (September): 580–594.

Burris, Val. 1986. "The Discovery of the New Middle Class." *Theory and Society* 15 (3): 317–349.

Cai, Yongshun. 2005. "China's Moderate Middle Class: The Case of Homeowners' Resistance." *Asian Survey* 45 (5): 777–799.

Campbell, Angus, Philip E. Converse, Warren E. Miller, and Donald E. Stokes. 1960. *The American Voter*. New York: John Wiley and Sons.

Cao, Yang. 2001. "Careers Inside Organizations: A Comparative Study of Promotion Determination in Reforming China." *Social Forces* 80 (2): 683–712.

Centers, Richard. 1949. *The Psychology of Social Classes*. Princeton, NJ: Princeton University Press.

Chen, An. 2002. "Capitalist Development, Entrepreneurial Class, and Democratization in China." *Political Science Quarterly* 117 (3): 401–422.

Chen, Feng. 1995. *Economic Transition and Political Legitimacy in Post-Mao China: Ideology and Reform*. Albany, NY: SUNY Press.

Chen, Jie. 2000. "Subjective Motivations for Mass Political Participation in Urban China." *Social Science Quarterly* 81: 645–662.

Chen, Jie. 2004. *Popular Political Support in Urban China*. Stanford, CA: Stanford University Press.

Chen, Jie. 2010. "Attitudes Toward Democracy and the Political Behavior of China's Middle Class." In *China's Emerging Middle Class*, ed. Cheng Li, 334–358. Washington, DC: Brookings Institution Press.

Chen, Jie, and Bruce Dickson. 2008. "Allies of the State: Democratic Support and Regime Support among China's Private Entrepreneurs." *China Quarterly* 196: 780–804.

Chen, Jie, and Bruce Dickson. 2010. *Allies of the State: Private Entrepreneurs and Democratic Change in China*. New Haven, CT: Yale University Press.

Chen, Jie, and Chunlong Lu. 2011. "Democratization and the Middle Class in China: The Middle Class's Attitudes Toward Democracy." *Political Research Quarterly* 64 (3): 705–719.

Chen, Jie, and Yang Zhong. 1998. "Defining the Political System of Post-Deng China: Emerging Public Support for a Democratic Political System." *Problems of Post-Communism* 45 (1): 30–42.

Chen, Jie, and Yang Zhong. 2000. "Valuation of Individual Liberty vs. Social Order Among Democratic Supporters: A Cross-Validation." *Political Research Quarterly* 53: 427–439.

Chen, Jie, and Yang Zhong. 2002. "Why Do People Vote in Semicompetitive Elections in China? A Reassessment of Voters' Subjective Motivations in Local People's Congress Elections." *Journal of Politics* 64: 178–197.

Chibber, Vivek. 2003. *Locked in Place: State Building and Late Industrialization in India*. Princeton, NJ: Princeton University Press.

Chiu, Rebecca L. H. 2001. "Commodification of Housing with Chinese Characteristics." *Policy Studies Review* 18 (1): 75–95.

Dahl, Robert A. 1971. *Polyarchy: Participation and Opposition*. New Haven, CT: Yale University Press.

Davis, Deborah S. 1992a. "Job Mobility in Post-Mao Cities: Increases on the Margins." *China Quarterly* 84: 1062–1085.

Davis, Deborah S. 1992b. "Skidding: Downward Mobility Among Children of the Maoist Middle Class." *Modern China* 18 (4): 410–437.

Davis, Deborah S. 1999. "Self-Employment in Shanghai: A Research Note." *China Quarterly* 157: 22–43.

Davis, Deborah S. 2000. "Social Class Transformation in Urban China: Training, Hiring, and Promoting Urban Professionals and Managers After 1949." *Modern China* 26 (3): 251–275.

Davis, Diane E. 2004. *Discipline and Development: Middle Classes and Prosperity in East Asia and Latin America*. New York: Cambridge University Press.

Derleth, James, and Daniel R. Koldyk. 2004. "The Shequ Experiment: Grassroots Political Reform in Urban China." *Journal of Contemporary China* 13 (41): 747–777

Dickson, Bruce. 2003. *Red Capitalist in China: The Party, Private Entrepreneurs, and Prospects for Political Change*. New York: Cambridge University Press.

Dickson, Bruce. 2008. *Wealth into Power: The Communist Party's Embrace of China's Private Sector*. New York: Cambridge University Press.

Dittmer, Lowell, and Lance Gore. 2001. "China Builds a Market Culture." *East Asia* 19 (3): 9–50.

Dolven, Ben. 2003. "A Home Revolt at Ground Level." *Far Eastern Economic Review* 166 (42): 35–37.

Easton, David. 1965. *A Systems Analysis of Political Life.* New York: John Wiley and Sons.

Easton, David. 1976. "Theoretical Approaches to Political Support." *Canadian Journal of Political Science* 9 (3): 431–448.

Englehart, Neil A. 2003. "Democracy and the Thai Middle Class." *Asian Survey* 43 (2): 253–279.

Erikson, Robert, and John H. Goldthorpe. 1992. *The Constant Flux: A Study of Class Mobility in Industrial Societies.* New York: Oxford University Press.

Eulau, Heinz. 1956a. "Identification with Class and Political Perspective." *Journal of Politics* 18 (2): 232–253.

Eulau, Heinz. 1956b. "Identification with Class and Political Role Behavior." *Public Opinion Quarterly* 20 (3): 515–529.

Evans, Peter. 1995. *Embedded Autonomy: State and Industrial Transformation.* Princeton, NJ: Princeton University Press.

Evans, Peter, Dietrich Rueschemeyer, and Theda Skocpol, eds. 1985. *Bringing the State Back In.* New York: Cambridge University Press.

Fan, Ren. 2005. "The Fight for Property Rights: Organizations to Protect Homeowners' Rights Are an Indication That Community Politics Are on the Rise." *Beijing Review* 48 (30): 34–35.

Fernandes, Leela. 2006. *India's New Middle Class: Democratic Politics in an Era of Economic Reform.* Minneapolis: University of Minnesota Press.

Finkel, Steven E., Edward N. Muller, and Mitchell Seligson. 1989. "Economic Crisis, Incumbent Performance, and Regime Support: A Comparison of Longitudinal Data from West Germany and Costa Rica." *British Journal of Political Science* 19 (July): 329–351.

Fowler, Floyd D. 1988. *Survey Research Methods.* Beverly Hills, CA: Sage Publications.

Fukuyama, Francis. 1993. "Capitalism & Democracy: The Missing Link." In *Capitalism, Socialism, and Democracy Revisited,* ed. Larry Diamond and Marc F. Plattner, 94–104. Baltimore: Johns Hopkins University Press.

Gallagher, Mary E. 2002. "'Reform and Openness' Why China's Economic Reform Have Delayed Democracy." *World Politics* 54 (3): 338–372.

Gerschenkron, Alexander. 1962. *Economic Backwardness in Historical Perspective: A Book of Essays.* Cambridge, MA: Belknap Press of Harvard University Press.

Gibson, James L. 1995. "The Resilience of Mass Support for Democratic Institutions and Processes in Nascent Russian and Ukrainian Democracies." In *Political Culture and Civil Society in Russia and the New States of Eurasia,* ed. Vladimir Tismaneanu, 53–111. Armonk, NY: M. E. Sharpe.

Gibson, James L., and Raymond M. Duch. 1993. "Emerging Democratic Values in Soviet Political Culture." In *Public Opinion and Regime Change,* ed. Arthur H. Miller, William M. Reisinger, and Vicki L. Hesli, 69–94. Boulder, CO: Westview Press.

Gibson, James L., Raymond M. Duch, and Kent L. Tedin. 1992. "Democratic Values and the Transformation of the Soviet Union." *Journal of Politics* 54 (2): 329–371.

Glassman, Ronald M. 1991. *China in Transition: Communism, Capitalism, and Democracy*. New York: Praeger.

Glassman, Ronald M. 1995. *The Middle Class and Democracy in Socio-Historical Perspective*. Leiden, The Netherlands: E. J. Brill.

Glassman, Ronald M. 1997. *The New Middle Class and Democracy in Global Perspective*. New York: St. Martin's Press; London: Macmillan Press.

Goodman, David G. 1996. "The People's Republic of China: The Party-State, Capitalist Revolution and New Entrepreneurs." In *The New Rich in Asia: Mobile Phones, McDonalds and Middle-Class Revolution*, ed. Richard Robison and David G. Goodman, 225–242. London: Routledge.

Goodman, David G. 1999. "The New Middle Class." In *The Paradox of China's Post-Mao Reforms*, ed. Merle Goldman and Roderick MacFarquhar, 241–261. Cambridge, MA: Harvard University Press.

Gupta, Dipankar. 2000. *Mistaken Modernity: India Between Worlds*. New Delhi: HarperCollins Publishers India.

Hadiz, Vedi R. 2004. "The Rise of Neo-Third Worldism? The Indonesian Trajectory and the Consolidation of Illiberal Democracy." *Third World Quarterly* 25 (1): 55–71.

Han, Sang-Jin. 2010. "Middle-Class Grassroots Identity and Participation in Citizen Initiatives, China and South Korea." In *China's Emerging Middle Class*, ed. Cheng Li, 264–290. Washington, DC: Brookings Institution Press.

Hattori, Tamio, and Tsuruyo Funatsu. 2003. "The Emergence of the Asian Middle Classes and Their Characteristics." *Developing Economies* 41 (2): 140–160.

Hattori, Tamio, Tsuruyo Funatsu, and Takashi Torii. 2003. "Introduction: The Emergence of the Asian Middle Classes and Their Characteristics." *Developing Economies* 41 (2): 129–139.

Hayes, Bernadette C. 1995. "The Impact of Class on Political Attitudes: A Comparative Study of Great Britain, West Germany, Australia, and the United States." *European Journal of Political Research* 27: 69–91.

Halpern, Nina P. 1991. "Economic Reform, Social Mobilization, and Democratization in Post-Mao China." In *Reform and Reaction in Post-Mao China: The Road to Tiananmen*, ed. Richard Baum. New York: Routledge.

Hsiao, Hsin-Huang Michael. 2010. "Placing China's Middle Class in the Asia-Pacific Context." In *China's Emerging Middle Class*, ed. Cheng Li, 245–263. Washington, DC: Brookings Institution Press.

Hsiao, Hsin-Huang Michael, and Hagen Koo. 1997. "The Middle Classes and Democratization." In *Consolidating the Third Wave Democracies*, ed. Larry Diamond et al., 312–333. Baltimore: Johns Hopkins University Press.

Hsiao, Hsin-Huang Michael, and Alvin Y. So. 1999. "The Making of the East Asian Middle Classes: The Five Propositions." In *East Asian Middle Classes in Comparative Perspective*, ed. Hsin-Huang Michael Hsiao, 3–49. Taipei: Institute of Ethnology, Academia Sinica.

Huntington, Samuel P. 1971. "The Change to Change." *Comparative Politics* 3: 283–322.

Huntington, Samuel P. 1991. *The Third Wave: Democratization in the Late Twentieth Century*. Norman: University of Oklahoma Press.

International Finance Corporation. 2000. *China's Emerging Private Enterprises: Prospects for the New Century*. Washington, DC: International Finance Corporation.

Jennings, M. Kent. 1997. "Political Participation in the Chinese Countryside." *American Political Science Review* 91: 361–372.

Jennings, M. Kent. 1998. "Gender and Political Participation in the Chinese Countryside." *Journal of Politics* 60 (November): 954–973.

Johnson, Dale L. 1985. "Class and Social Development: Toward a Comparative and Historical Social Science." In *Middle Classes in Dependent Countries*, ed. Dale L. Johnson, 13–41. Beverly Hills, CA: Sage Publications.

Johnston, Alastair Iain. 2004. "Chinese Middle Class Attitudes Towards International Affairs: Nascent Liberalization?" *China Quarterly* 179: 603–628.

Jones, David Martin. 1998. "Democratization, Civil Society, and Illiberal Middle Class Culture in Pacific Asia." *Comparative Politics* 30 (2): 147–169.

Kahl, Joseph Alan. 1957. *The American Class Structure*. New York: Rinehart.

Katzenstein, Peter. 1985. "Small Nations in an Open International Economy: The Converging Balance of State and Society in Switzerland and Austria." In *Bringing the State Back In,* eds. Peter Evans, Dietrich Rueschemeyer, and Theda Skocpol, 227–256. New York: Cambridge University Press.

Kharas, Homi, and Geoffrey Gertz. 2010. "The Global Middle Class: A Crossover from West to East." In *China's Emerging Middle Class*, ed. Cheng Li, 32–54. Washington, DC: Brookings Institution Press.

Kimura, Masataka. 2003. "The Emergence of the Middle Classes and Political Change in the Philippines." *Developing Economies* 41 (2): 264–284.

Kohli, Atul. 2004. *State-Directed Development: Political Power and Industrialization in the Global Periphery*. Princeton, NJ: Princeton University Press.

Koo, Hagen. 1991. "Middle Classes, Democratization, and Class Formation: The Case of South Korea." *Theory and Society* 20 (4): 485–509.

LaFraniere, Sharon. 2011. "Alarmed by Independent Candidates, Chinese Authorities Crack Down." *New York Times* (December 4, 2011).

http://www.nytimes.com/2011/12/05/world/asia/china-clamps-down-on-even-a-by-the-book-campaign.html?ref=asia.

Lam, Peng Er. 1999. "Singapore: Rich State, Illiberal Regime." In *Driven by Growth: Political Change in the Asia-Pacific Region*, ed. James W. Morley, 255–274. New York: M. E. Sharpe.

Lam, Tao-chiu, and Jerry L. Perry. 2001. "Services Organizations in China: Reforms and Institutional Constraints." *Policy Studies Review* 18 (1): 16–35.

Lane, Robert E. 1959. *Political Life: Why People Get Involved in Politics*. Glencoe, IL: Free Press.

Lee, Ching Kwan. 2000. "Pathways of Labor Insurgency." In *Chinese Society: Change, Conflict and Resistance*, ed. Elizabeth J. Perry and Mark Selden, 41–61. London: Routledge.

Li, Chunling. 2003. "Zhongguo dangdai zhongchan jieceng de goucheng ji bili" [The Composition and Size of China's Contemporary Middle Class]. *Zhongguo renkou kexue [Chinese Population Science]* 2003 (6): 25–32.

Li, He. 2003. "Middle Class: Friends or Foes to Beijing's New Leadership." *Journal of Chinese Political Science* 8 (1&2): 87–100.

Liang, Xiaoshen. 2011. *Zhongguo shehui gejiceng feixi [An Analysis of China's Social Classes]*. Beijing: Culture and Art Publishing House.

Lin, Nan, and Wen Xie. 1988. "Occupational Prestige in Urban China." *American Journal of Sociology* 93: 793–832.

Lipset, Seymour M. 1959. "Some Social Requisites of Democracy: Economic Development and Political Legitimacy." *American Political Science Review* 53 (1): 69–105.

Lipset, Seymour M. 1968. "Stratification: Social Class." In *International Encyclopedia of the Social Science*, Vol. 15, 296–316. New York: Collier Macmillan.

Lipset, Seymour M. 1981. *Political Man: The Social Bases of Politics* (1st ed., 1959). Baltimore: Johns Hopkins University Press.

Lipset, Seymour, and Reinhard Bendix. 1959. *Social Mobility in Industrial Society*. Berkeley: University of California Press.

Locke, John. 1967. *Two Treatises of Government*. London: Cambridge University Press.

Lu, Xueyi, ed. 2002. *Dangdai zhongguo shehui jieceng yanjiu baogao [Research Report on Contemporary China's Social Classes]*. Beijing: Shehui kexue wenxian chubanshe.

Lu, Xueyi, ed. 2004. *Dangdai zhongguo shehui liudong [Social Mobility in Contemporary China]*. Beijing: Shehui kexue wenxian chubanshe.

Lu, Xueyi, ed. 2010. *Dangdai zhongguo shehui jiegou [Social Structure of Comtemporary China]*. Beijing: Shehui kexue wenxian chubanshe.

Lu, Ya-li. 1991. "Political Development in the Republic of China." In *Democracy and Development in East Asia: Taiwan, South Korea, and the Philippines*, ed. Thomas W. Robinson, 35–47. Washington, DC: AEI Press.

Luebbert, Gregory M. 1991. *Liberalism, Fascism, or Social Democracy: Social Classes and the Political Origins of Regimes in Interwar Europe*. New York: Oxford University Press.

Luedde-Neurath, Richard. 1986. *Import Controls and Export-Oriented Development: A Reassessment of the South Korea Case.* Boulder, CO: Westview.

Macridis, Roy C. 1992. *Contemporary Political Ideologies: Movements and Regimes.* New York: Harper Collins.

Manion, Melanie. 1994. "Survey Research in the Study of Contemporary China: Learning from Local Samples." *China Quarterly* 139: 741–765.

Manion, Melanie. 1996. "The Electoral Connection in the Chinese Countryside." *American Political Science Review* 90: 736–748.

Mao, Wen. 2010. 探访中国"中产"群体:都是些房奴车奴卡奴孩奴 [Study on China's "Middle Class" Group: All Working like Slaves for Their Houses, Cars, and Children]. *Zhongxin Web* (September 9, 2010). http://news.powerapple.com/articles/108641.

Marsh, Alan, and Max Kaase. 1979. "Background of Political Action." In *Political Action: Mass Participation in Five Western Democracies*, ed. Samuel H. Barnes et al., 97–136. Beverley Hills, CA: Sage.

McCormick, Barrett. 1990. *Political Reform in Post-Mao China: Democracy and Bureaucracy in a Leninist State.* Berkeley: University of California Press.

McCormick, Barrett L. 1996. "China's Leninist Parliament and Public Sphere: A Comparative Analysis." In *China after Socialism: in the Footsteps of Eastern Europe or East Asia?* Ed. Barrett L. McCormick and Jonathan Unger. Armonk, NY: M.E. Sharpe. Pp. 29–53.

Migdal, Joel S. 2001. *State in Society: Studying How Sates and Societies Transform and Constitute One Another.* New York: Cambridge University Press.

Milbrath, Lester W. 1977. *Political Participation: How and Why Do People Get Involved in Politics?* 2nd ed. Chicago: Rand McNally College Publishing.

Mills, C. Wright. 1953. *White Collar: The American Middle Classes.* New York: Oxford University Press.

Mitchell, Timothy. 1991. "The Limits of the State: Beyond Statist Approaches and Their Critics." *American Political Science Review* 85: 77–96.

Moore, Barrington. 1966. *Social Origins of Dictatorship and Democracy: Lord and Peasant in the Making of the Modern World.* Boston: Beacon Press.

Muller, Edward N. 1977. "Behavioral Correlates of Political Support." *American Political Science Review* 71 (June): 454–467.

Muller, Edward N. 1997. "Economic Determinants of Democracy." In *Inequality, Democracy, and Economic Development*, ed. Manus I. Midlarsky, 133–155. New York: Cambridge University Press.

Muller, Edward N., and Thomas O. Jukam, 1977. "On the Meaning of Political Support." *American Political Science Review* 71 (December): 1561–1595.

Muller, Edward N., Mitchell A. Seligson, and Hung-der Fu. 1989. "Land Inequality and Political Violence." *American Political Science Review* 83 (June): 577–587.

Muller, Edward N., and Carol J. Williams. 1980. "Dynamics of Political Support-Alienation." *Comparative Political Studies* 13 (1): 33–59.

Nathan, Andrew J. 1990. *China's Crisis: Dilemma of Reform and Prospects for Democracy.* New York: Columbia University Press.

Nathan, Andrew J. 1997. *China's Transition.* New York: Columbia University Press.

Nathan, Andrew J. 2007. "Political Culture and Regime Support in Asia." Paper presented at the conference on "The Future of U.S.-China Relations" at University of Southern California, April 20–21, 2007.

Nathan, Andrew J. 2008. "China's Political Trajectory: What Are the Chinese Saying?" In *China's Changing Political Landscape: Prospects for Democracy,* ed. Cheng Li, 25–43. Washington, DC: Brookings Institution Press.

National People's Congress (of the PRC). 1982. *The Constitution of the People's Republic of China.* Beijing Review 52 (December 27): 10–52.

Nathan, Andrew J. 1985. *Chinese Democracy.* New York: Alfred A. Knopf.

Naughton, Barry. 2007. *The Chinese Economy: Transitions and Growth.* Cambridge, MA: MIT Press.

Nee, Victor. 1989. "A Theory of Market Transition: From Redistribution to Markets in State Socialism." *American Sociological Review* 54: 663–681.

Nee, Victor. 1991. "Social Inequalities in Reforming State Socialism: Between Redistribution and Markets in China." *American Sociological Review* 56: 267–282.

Nee, Victor. 1996. "The Emergence of a Market Society: Changing Mechanisms of Stratification in China." *American Journal of Sociology* 101 (4): 908–949.

Nee, Victor, and Rebecca Matthews. 1996. "Market Transition and Societal Transformation in Reforming State Socialism." *Annual Review of Sociology* 22: 401–435.

Nie, Norman H., G. Bingham Powell, Jr., and Kenneth Prewitt. 1969. "Social Structure and Political Participation: Developmental Relationships, Part I and II." *American Political Science Review* 63: 361–378 and 808–832.

O'Brien, Kevin J. 1990. *Reform without Liberalization: China's National People's Congress and the Politics of Institutional Change.* New York: Cambridge University Press.

O'Brien, Kevin J., and Rachel E. Stern. 2008. "Introduction: Studying Contention in Contemporary China." In *Popular Protest in China,* ed. Kevin J. O'Brien, 11–25. Cambridge, MA: Harvard University Press.

Ogden, Suzanne. 2002. *Inklings of Democracy in China.* Cambridge, MA: Harvard University Asia Center and distributed by Harvard University Press.

Oi, Jean C. 1999. *Rural China Takes Off: Institutional Foundations of Economic Reform.* Berkeley and Los Angeles: University of California Press.

Oppenheimer, Martin. 1985. *White Collar Politics.* New York: Monthly Review Press.

Owensby, Brian. 1999. *Intimate Ironies: Modernity and the Making of Middle Class Lives in Brazil*. Stanford, CA: Stanford University Press.

Packenham, Robert. 1992. *The Dependency Movement: Scholarship and Politics in Development Studies*. Cambridge, MA: Harvard University Press.

Parish, William L. 1984. "Destratification in China." In *Class and Social Stratification in Post-Revolution China*, ed. James L. Watson, 84–120. Cambridge: Cambridge University Press.

Parish, William L., and Ethan Michelson. 1996. "Politics and Markets: Dual Transformations." *American Journal of Sociology* 101 (4): 1042–1059.

Pearson, Margaret M. 1997. *China's New Business Elite: The Political Consequences of Economic Reform*. Berkeley: University of California Press.

Pei, Minxin. 2006. *China's Trapped Transition: The Limits of Developmental Autocracy*. Cambridge, MA: Harvard University Press.

Poulantzas, Nicos. 1975. *Classes in Contemporary Capitalism*. London: New Left Books.

Przeworski, Adam, and Fernando Limongi, 1997. "Modernization: Theories and Facts." *World Politics* 49: 155–183.

Pye, Lucian W. 1992. *The Spirit of Chinese Politics*. Cambridge, MA: Harvard University Press.

Qiu, Zeqi, 2004. *Dangdai zhongguo shehui fenceng zhuangkuang de bianqian [The Changes of Social Stratification in Contemporary China]*. Heibei, China: Hebei daxue chubanshe.

Read, Benjamin L. 2004. "Democratizing the Neighborhood? New Private Housing and Home-Owner Self-Organization in Urban China." *China Journal* 49: 31–59.

Rodan, Garry. 1993. "The Growth of Singapore's Middle Class and its Political Significance." In *Singapore Changes Guard: Social, Political and Economic Directions in the 1990s*, ed. Garry Rodan, 52–71. Melbourne: Longman Cheshire.

Rona-Tas, Akos. 1994. "The First Shall Be Last? Entrepreneurship and Communist Cadres in the Transition from Socialism." *American Journal of Sociology* 100 (1): 40–69.

Rose, Richard, William Mishler, and Neil Munro. 2011. *Popular Support for an Undemocratic Regime: The Changing Views of Russians*. New York: Cambridge University Press.

Rostow, Walt W. 1960. *Stages of Economic Growth: A Non-Communist Manifesto,* 1st ed. Cambridge: Cambridge University Press.

Rostow, Walt W. 1991. *Stages of Economic Growth: A Non-Communist Manifesto,* 3rd ed. New York: Cambridge University Press.

Rueschemeyer, Dietrich, and Peter Evans. 1985. "The State and Economic Transformation: Toward an Analysis of the Conditions Underlying Effective Intervention." In *Bringing the State Back In,* ed. Peter Evans, Dietrich Rueschemeyer, and Theda Skocpol, 44–77. New York: Cambridge University Press.

Rueschemeyer, Dietrich, Evelyne Huber Stephens, and John D. Stephens. 1992. *Capitalist Development and Democracy*. Chicago: University of Chicago Press.

Scalapino, Robert A. 1998. "Current Trends and Future Prospects." *Journal of Democracy* 9: 35–40.

Schmitter, Philippe. 1974. "Still the Century of Corporatism?" *Review of Politics* 36 (1): 85–131.

Schumpeter, Joseph A. 1947. *Capitalism, Socialism, and Democracy*. New York: Harper.

Seligson, Mitchell A., and Edward N. Muller. 1987. "Democratic Stability and Economic Crisis: Costa Rica, 1978–1983." *International Studies Quarterly* 31 (September): 301–326.

Sherkat, Darren, and T. Jean Blocker. 1994. "The Political Development of Sixties' Activities: Identifying the Influence of Class, Gender, and Socialization on Protest Participation." *Social Forces* 72 (3): 821–842.

Shi, Tianjian. 1997. *Political Participation in Beijing*. Cambridge, MA: Harvard University Press.

Shi, Tianjian. 1999a. "Village Committee Elections in China: Institutionalist Tactic for Democracy." *World Politics* 51 (3): 385–412.

Shi, Tianjian. 1999b. "Economic Development and Village Elections in Rural China." *Journal of Contemporary China* 8 (22): 425–442.

Shi, Weimin, and Lei Jingxuan. 1999. *Zhijie xuanju: system and procedure* (Direct elections: the system and procedure). Beijing: Chinese Academy of Social Sciences Press.

Shin, Eui Hang. 1999. "Social Change, Political Elections, and the Middle Class in Korea." *East Asia: An International Quarterly* 17 (3): 28–60.

Shirk, Susan L. 1984. "The Decline of Virtuocracy in China." In *Class and Social Stratification in Post-Revolution China*, ed. James L. Watson, 56–83. Cambridge: Cambridge University Press.

Shwarz, Adam. 1994. *A Nation in Waiting: Indonesia in the 1990s*. Boulder, CO: Westview Press.

Skocpol, Theda. 1985. "Bringing the State Back In: Strategies of Analysis in Current Research." In *Bringing the State Back In*, ed. Peter Evans, Dietrich Rueschemeyer, and Theda Skocpol, 3–43. New York: Cambridge University Press.

So, Alvin Y. 2003. "The Changing Pattern of Classes and Class Conflict in China." *Journal of Contemporary Asia* 33 (3): 363–376.

So, Alvin Y. 2004. "The Middle Class in Asia-Pacific: Second-Phase Research and Future Trajectory." *Asian Perspective* 28 (2): 263–275.

So, Alvin Y., and Ludmilla Kwitko. 1990. "The New Middle Class and the Democratic Movement in Hong Kong." *Journal of Contemporary Asia* 20: 384–398.

Solinger, Dorothy. 1992. "Urban Entrepreneurs and the State: The Merger of State and Society." In *State and Society in China: The Consequences of Reform*, ed. Arthur Rosenbaum, 121–141. Boulder, CO: Westview Press.

Solinger, Dorothy. 2008. "Business Groups: For or Against the Regime." In *Political Change in China: Comparisons with Taiwan,* ed. Bruce Gilley and Larry Diamond, 95–114. Boulder, CO: Lynne Rienner.

South Weekly. 2010. "一个" 中产" 家庭的通胀焦虑" [The Anxiety of a Middle-Class Family over Inflation]. *South Weekly* (July 23, 2010).

Stepan, Alfred. 1985. "State Power and the Strength of Civil Society in the Southern Cone of Latin America." In *Bringing the State Back In,* ed. Peter Evans, Dietrich Rueschemeyer, and Theda Skocpol, 317–346. New York: Cambridge University Press.

Stephens, Evelyne Huber. 1989. "Capitalist Development and Democracy in South America." *Politics and Society* 17 (3): 281–352.

Sundhaussen, Ulf. 1991. "Democracy and the Middle Classes: Reflections on Political Development." *Australian Journal of Politics and History* 37: 100–117.

Tamura, Keiko T. 2003. "The Emergence and Political Consciousness of the Middle Class in Singapore." *Developing Economies* 41 (2): 184–200.

Tang, Wenfang. 2005. *Public Opinion and Political Change in China.* Stanford, CA: Stanford University Press.

Tang, Wenfang, and William L. Parish. 2000. *Chinese Urban Life under Reform: The Changing Social Contract.* Cambridge: Cambridge University Press.

Pempel, T. J. 1999 (ed.). The Politics of the Asian Economic Crisis. Cornell University Press.

Thompson, Mark R. 2004. "Pacific Asia after 'Asian Values': Authoritarianism, Democracy, and 'Good Governance.'" *Third World Quarterly* 25 (6): 1079–1095.

Tilly, Charles. 1985. "War Making and State Making as Organized Crime." In *Bringing the State Back In,* ed. Peter Evans, Dietrich Rueschemeyer, and Theda Skocpol, 169–191. New York: Cambridge University Press.

Tomba, Luigi. 2004. "Creating an Urban Middle Class: Social Engineering in Beijing." *China Journal* 51: 1–26.

Torii, Takashi. 2003. "The Mechanism for State-Led Creation of Malaysia's Middle Classes." *Developing Economies* 41 (2): 221–242.

Townsend, James R. 1967. *Political Participation in Communist China.* Berkeley and Los Angeles: University of California Press.

Tsai, Kellee S. 2002. *Back Alley Banking: Private Entrepreneurs in China.* Ithaca, NY: Cornell University Press.

Tsai, Kellee S. 2005. "Capitalists Without a Class: Political Diversity Among Private Entrepreneurs in China." *Comparative Political Studies* 38 (9): 1130–1158.

Tsai, Kellee S. 2006. "Adaptive Informal Institutions and Endogenous Institutional Change in China." *World Politics* 59: 116–141.

Tsai, Kellee S. 2007. *Capitalism Without Democracy: The Private Sector in Contemporary China.* Ithaca, NY: Cornell University Press.

Unger, Jonathan, and Anita Chan. 1995. "China, Corporatism, and the East Asian Model." *Australian Journal of Chinese Affairs* 33: 29–53.

Verba, Sidney, and Norman H. Nie. 1972. *Participation in America: Political Democracy and Social Equality.* New York: Harper and Row Publishers.

Verba, Sidney, Norman Nie, and Jae-on Kim. 1978. *Participation and Political Equality: A Seven-Nation Comparison.* New York: Cambridge University Press.

Wade, Robert. 1990. *Governing the Market: Economic Theory and the Role of Government in East Asian Industrialization.* Princeton, NJ: Princeton University Press.

Walder, Andrew G., ed. 1995a. *The Waning of the Communist State: Economic Origins of Political Decline in China and Hungary.* Berkeley: University of California Press.

Walder, Andrew G. 1995b. "Career Mobility and the Communist Political Order." *American Sociological Review* 60: 309–328.

Walder, Andrew G. 1989. "Social Change in Post-Revolution China." *Annual Review of Sociology* 15: 405–424.

Walder, Andrew G., Bobai Li, and Donald J. Treiman. 2000. "Politics and Life Chances in a State Socialist Regime: Dual Career Paths into the Urban Chinese Elite, 1949 to 1996." *American Sociological Review* 65 (2): 191–209.

Walsh, Katherine Cramer, M. Kent Jennings, and Laura Stoker. 2004. "The Effects of Social Class Identification on Participatory Orientations Towards Government." *British Journal of Political Science* 34: 469–495.

Wang, James C.F. 1999. *Contemporary Chinese Politics.* Upper Saddle River, NJ: Prentice Hall.

Wang, Yaping, and Alan Murie. 1996. "The Process of Commercialisation of Urban Housing in China." *Urban Studies* 33 (6): 971–989.

Wang, Zhongtian. 1998. *Xingde bi'an: Zouxiang 21st shiji de zhongguo minzhu* (A new horizon: marching toward the Chinese democracy in the 21st century). Beijing: The Party School of the CCP's Central Committee Press.

Weston, Timothy. 2000. "China's Labor Woes: Will the Workers Crash the Party?" In *China: Beyond the Headlines*, ed. Timothy Weston and Lionel M. Jensen, 245–271. Lanham, MD: Rowman and Littlefield Publishers.

White, Gordon, and Robert Wade. 1988. "Developmental States and Markets in East Asia: An Introduction." In *Developmental States in East Asia*, ed. Gordon White, 1–29. London: Macmillan.

Whyte, Martin King. 1975. "Inequality and Stratification in China." *China Quarterly* 64: 684–711.

Whyte, Martin King. 1985. "The Politics of Life Chances in the People's Republic of China." In *Power and Policy in the PRC*, ed. Yu-ming Shaw, 244–265. Boulder, CO, and London: Westview Press.

Whyte, Martin King. 1999. "The Changing Role of Workers." In *The Paradox of China's Post-Mao Reforms*, ed. Merle Goldman and Roderick MacFarquhar, 173–196. Cambridge, MA: Harvard University Press.

Woo-Cumings, Meredith, ed. 1999. *The Developmental State.* Ithaca, NY: Cornell University Press.

Wright, Erik Olin. 1997. *Class Counts: Comparative Studies in Class Analysis.* Cambridge: Cambridge University Press.

Wright, Teresa. 2010. *Accepting Authoritarianism: State-Society Relations in China's Reform Era.* Stanford, CA: Stanford University Press

Wu, Xiaogang. 2002. "Work Units and Income Inequality: The Effect of Market Transition in Urban China." *Social Forces* 80 (3): 1069–1099.

Wu, Xiaogang, and Donald J. Treiman. 2004. "The Household Registration System and Social Stratification in China: 1955–1996." *Demography* 41 (2): 363–384.

Xiao, Gongqin. 2003. "The Rise of the Technocrats." *Journal of Democracy* 14 (1): 59–65.

Xiao, Wentao. 2001. "Zhongguo zhongjian jieceng de xianzhuang he weilai fazhan" [The Current Situation and Future Development of China's Middle Stratum]. *Shehuixue yanjiu [Sociological Research]* 2001 (3): 93–98.

Yang, Jisheng. 2011. *Zhonguo dangdai shehui jiecen fengxi [An Analysis of China's Contemporary Social Classes].* Nanchang, Jiangxi: Jiangxi Higher Education Publisher.

Zhang, Li. 2010. *In Search of Paradise: Middle-Class Living in a Chinese Metropolis.* Ithaca, NY: Cornell University Press.

Zhang, Wei. 2005. *Chongtu yu bianshu: Zhongguo shehui zhongjian jieceng zhengzhi fenxi [Conflict and Uncertainty: Political Analysis of the Middle Stratum in Chinese Society].* Beijing: Shehui kexue wenxian chubanshe.

Zheng, Hangsheng, and Lulu Li. 2004. *Dangdai zhongguo chengshi shehui jiegou [Social Structure of the Cities in Contemporary China].* Beijing: Zhongguo renmin daxue chubanshe.

Zheng, Yongnian. 2004a. *Globalization and State Transformation in China.* Cambridge: Cambridge University Press.

Zheng, Yongnian. 2004b. *Will China Become Democratic? Elite, Class and Regime Change.* London: Eastern Universities Press.

Zheng, Yongnian. 2011. *Baowei shehui [Society Must be Defended].* Hangzhou, Zhejiang: Zhenjiang People's Press.

Zhong, Yang, and Jie Chen. 2002. "To Vote or Not to Vote: An Analysis of Peasants' Participation in Chinese Village Elections." *Comparative Political Studies* 35 (6): 686–712.

Zhou, Xiaohong. 2002. "Zhongchan jieji: heyi keneng yu heyi kewei?" [Middle Class: What are Possibilities and Capabilities?]. *Jiangsu shehui kexue [Jiangsu Journal of Social Sciences]* 6: 37–45.

Zhou, Xiaohong. 2005. *Zhongguo zhongchan jieceng diaocha [Survey of the Chinese Middle Class].* Beijing: Shehui kexue wenxian chubanshe.

Zhou, Xueguang. 2000. "Economic Transformation and Income Inequality in Urban China: Evidence from Panel Data." *American Journal of Sociology* 105 (4): 1135–1174.

Zhou, Xueguang. 2004. *The State and Life Chances in Urban China.* Cambridge: Cambridge University Press.

Zhou, Xueguang, Nancy Brandon Tuma, and Phyllis Moen. 1996. "Stratification Dynamics under State Socialism: the Case of Urban China, 1949–1993." *Social Forces* 74 (3): 759–796.

Zipp, John F. 1986. "Social Class and Social Liberalism." *Sociological Forum* 1 (2): 301–329.

Index